Catch the *Fun*

Catch the *Laughter*

Catch the *Joy*

— *The Rod of Faith* —

(And them ain't no small fish either)

by
Veda Boyd
and Laurette Connelly

CATCH THE FUN
CATCH THE LAUGHTER
CATCH THE JOY

Copyright © 2003
All rights reserved.

"Odds and Ends," a duo ministry speaking team, presents to you this book on JOY—the same subject from two godly perspectives.

Catch the Fun, Catch the Laughter, Catch the Joy consists of stories combined with Biblical principals, personal humor, and applications for an enduring joyride through life.

Duplication of ideas, diversity of sources, and writing styles, are intended for the purpose of enhancing the message—another way of saying: "We didn't have time to compare notes."

Like a delayed education, it is never too late to learn, so grab the rod of faith and catch the fun, catch the laughter, catch the joy!
GO FISH!

Library of Congress Number: 2003110264
International Standard Book Number: 1-930353-83-9

Printed 2003
Masthof Press
219 Mill Road
Morgantown, PA 19543-9516

Dedication

We believe *Catch the Fun, Catch the Laughter, Catch the Joy* should be appropriately dedicated to "Friendship," recognizing God's sovereignty, not only in the universe, but also in the lives of those who call Him Lord.

We dedicate this book to our friendship, and to the friendships of others. Jesus is the architect of our friendship and the wings of our faith. He is author and finisher of our lives. A friend will come along side of you in the good and bad times and will call you into accountability with unconditional love and encouragement.

We are thankful for friendships and for friend-shifts, as God moves us on to grow spiritually and to depend more and more on Him. Friendship is a gift from God, a good gift, and to that we dedicate *Catch the Fun, Catch the Laughter, Catch the Joy*.

Table of Contents

Dedication iii
Preface vi
Notes vii
Acknowledgements viii

Chapter 1   . . . Free to Laugh 1
Chapter 2   Did Jesus Laugh? 11
Chapter 3   Benefits of Laughter 23
Chapter 4   To Laugh or Not to Laugh 37
Chapter 5   One Size Fits All 45
Chapter 6   Suppose I'm Not Funny 55
Chapter 7   Now Ain't That Funny 63
Chapter 8   A Song in the Night 73
Chapter 9   The Staying Power of Joy 83
Chapter 10   Joyful Journey Home 95

Preface

Out of genuine concern for protecting the Word of God and in order to avoid even a hint of irreverence, we feel it is necessary to reiterate that the chapter on Jesus' laughter is written only as a reflection of our thoughts on what may have been. These are merely suggestions to be considered. Only the Bible quotations in this book are to be taken as inspired and inerrant.

Sitting on my desktop, (Laurette) under a sheet of clear plexiglass is a picture of Jesus laughing out loud. Granted it's not a candid photograph, nor do I believe Jesus looked anything like that picture. But I do expect that if the paparazzi had been following Him around snapping His every move, sooner or later, they would have caught Him in the act of laughing.

Nowhere in Scripture are we told that Jesus laughed and some have even suggested that He did not. Ancient writings simply did not include laughter as part of the text. We do read about God laughing in the Old Testament but always as a means of warning. However, any serious student of the Bible would have to admit that Jesus indeed did laugh. To say anything different would be farcical. Incidentally, the Bible never says that Jesus took baths either—but He obviously did. Whether Jesus laughed or not has no relevance to salvation, it's just something to consider in our understanding of the need for the healing benefits of laughter in our own spiritual walk.

Notes

Source information regarding the benefits of laughter: Michael Miller, M.D., Director of the Center for Preventive Cardiology at the University of Maryland School of Medicine, quoted in an article by Michelle Weinstein, Web Site Writer for the University of Maryland Medical System.

Judy Goldblum-Carlton, a humor therapist at the University of Maryland Hospital for Children's Division of Pediatric Hematology/Oncology, and quoted in an article by Michelle Weinstein, Web Site Writer for the University of Maryland.

Dr. Clifford Kuhn, M.D., professor of psychiatry at the University of Louisville School of Medicine at Humana Live Events —March 12, 2001.

Acknowledgements

Tamara Good, a recent graduate of Penn State University, was born in Jos, Nigeria and spent her formative years primarily in Yaounde, Cameroon. She currently lives in Elizabethtown, PA with her husband and their little African Bushdog, Zoey. Without Tamara, this work would still be on the computer undergoing endless revisions and blank stares at the screen. We pray she will receive special blessings for the time and effort she devoted to editing *Catch the Fun, Catch the Laughter, Catch the Joy*.

Kim Robson, cover designer for *Catch the Fun, Catch the Laughter, Catch the Joy* is an accomplished artist from New Cumberland, PA. Kim is married and has two children. She is well known in the Central Pennsylvania area for her hand painted wall murals as well as her serious and whimsical subjects. Her "not for sale" contemporary painting of the Harrisburg Capitol Building remains the focus of numerous art collectors.

CHAPTER ONE

...Free to Laugh...

Veda Boyd

*"If you aren't allowed to laugh in heaven,
I don't want to go there."*
- Martin Luther (1483-1546)

The freedom to laugh began at the foot of an old rugged cross, when Jesus took our condemnation for sin upon Himself. That is why, every time we laugh, we should think about the price that was paid for that freedom, a thought that should make laughter all the more precious to those of us who have been set free in Christ.

"Therefore there is now no condemnation for those who are in Christ Jesus. For the law of the Spirit of life in Christ Jesus has set you free from the law of sin and of death." (Romans 8:1-2)

When my children were small, one of their favorite toys was the infamous Mr. Potato Head . . . today, it's Mr. Computer Head! (When did all the fun toys go and the frustrating replacements take over?) When Mr. Potato's head was misplaced, broken, or just not interesting, my children would create a solemn looking Mr. Potato face by taking the eyes, nose, and mouth from the game-box and affixing them to a real Idaho Potato. Often, I would think, as I feigned interest in their creative potato-art, *I know that person.* When I became a Christian, and thought about those solemn potato faces, I thought, *yes, I do know that person and they claim to be a believer in Jesus.*

Have you ever heard someone whistling a happy tune, even though they look like they have just swallowed half a lemon? I have. I have also heard an acclaimed believer in Jesus say, "I am just so happy in the Lord" even though they appeared to have just swallowed the other half of the whistler's lemon! The Bible says that one of the fruits of the Spirit is JOY, not lemons! *"But the fruit of the Spirit is love, JOY, peace, patience, kindness, goodness, faithfulness, gentleness, self-control . . . ." (Galatians 5:22)*

"A joyful heart is good medicine, but a broken spirit dries up the bones." (Proverbs 17:22) If you read that verse every time it appears in this book, you should have it memorized by the last chapter, and that's a good thing!

We would not ordinarily use the word slavery to describe perpetually unhappy looking people, and we especially avoid its use when referring to Christian brothers and sisters. Christians are not slaves to negativism or pessimism . . . or are they?

In lieu of joy, some believers convey spirituality and piety with a sad countenance, a custom I rarely read about in the Scriptures. I find it impossible to picture the disciples of Jesus a dispirited bunch. The disciples were not a pious group of clergymen. As a matter of fact, most of us would have balked at Jesus' choice of companions. They were not distinguished citizens of their time. But I believe, along with the hurts and disappointments His friends sometimes caused Him, they encouraged Jesus.

What is it that holds Christians back from their freedom to express JOY?

I once attended a seminar called, "Breaking Free" by Beth Moore. The title of the seminar made me think of people in bondage, slaves behind bars of unforgiveness, unconfessed sin and non-scriptural based traditions—accused of first-degree joy-less-ness . . . and found guilty! How sad, what a way to redeem the time!

As believers in Jesus, we are not only free to laugh and experience the "joy" in "enjoy," we are to go one step further and "count it all joy," even when we are facing trials. *"Count it all joy, my brethren, when you encounter various trials, knowing that the testing of your faith produces endurance . . ." (James 1:2-3)*

Abraham Lincoln said: "With the fearful strain that is on me night and day, if I did not laugh I should die."

People haven't changed much, have they? Laughter is still a useful weapon against defeat, depression and discouragement—its benefits are endless and free of charge.

Put the word FREE on a shelf in a store, in front of any grocery item, or even on a piece of furniture you labored to carry out to your front lawn (a less than desirable piece of furniture the garbage men wouldn't even want) and it disappears—overnight! But put the word FREE on Salvation, and suddenly we work like slaves to get or earn it; then once we think we have it, we quickly begin to act like we lost it!

Our faith in God, and in His Son, Jesus, has freed us to laugh—to live with joy in our hearts—and to keep our minds occupied by beautiful thoughts.

"Finally, brethren, whatever is true, whatever is honorable, whatever is right, whatever is pure, whatever is lovely, whatever is of good repute, if there is any excellence and if anything worthy of praise, dwell on these things." (Philippians 4:8)

If your morning begins with complaining, either about the weather, your family or your job, I can almost guarantee, that attitude will follow you like a shadow through the entire day.

We have no excuse to look like we've lost our best friend (unless we have lost our best friend), but we have many reasons to display on our face the joy that is in our hearts.

To quote Tim Hansel, words I discovered on the Internet (my grown-up Potato Head toy), "Laughter adds richness, texture, and color to otherwise ordinary days. It is a gift, a choice, a discipline, and an art."

I believe laughter should do for others what painting all my dark cottage walls antique white, did for me: it instantly brightened up my world, even before it had dried! It was as though someone had turned on all the lights, and for the first time since living in that cottage, I discovered there were actually daylight hours in my allotted twenty-four.

The natural joy of eternal security promised to those of us who believe in Jesus should bring a glow to our lives that not only lights up our life, but it should change how we talk, how we walk and how we love. It should also affect our attitude toward others.

We have been given so many wonderful promises, promises that should enable us to enjoy a vibrant life now! Our eternal happiness should begin on this earth and be completed and fulfilled when we enter heaven. If you are a believer in Jesus, and you do not embrace joy on earth, you have missed the shadow of things to come. Heaven will be joy-filled and our privilege or liberty, to experience that joy begins on earth. If we are following the One who is joy personified, an inseparable relationship, surely, His joy will be our joy, and His heartaches will be our heartaches.

"My sheep hear My voice, and I know them, and they follow Me; and I give eternal life to them, and they will never perish; and no one will snatch them out of the Father's hand." (John 10:28)

Some, who read that verse, will not want to hear what God is saying, because their joy and their eternal certainties have depended so long on other things: On other people, on themselves, and most often on their accomplishments and good works.

If someone paid an extravagant price on a gift for you, would you receive it with sadness? No, you would more than likely exclaim, "Oh, you shouldn't have!" You would appreciate that gift and you would love the giver for thinking so highly of you when he or she replies, "Oh, but I wanted to!" Jesus paid the ultimate price in order to give you and me the gift of eternal life, and neither you, nor I, had to pay one red cent for it. We just have to accept the price He paid, by faith, and allow our relationship with Jesus to change us from one of unholy living, to one of holy happiness. Yet, some Christians look like their salvation was just stolen by a thief in the night. Or maybe I'm just plain wrong. Maybe Christians are just hoarding their joy, for fear of losing it. That's not the God I know. The God the Bible speaks about keeps on giving. You can't out-give Him. You won't run out of joy if you are in tune with the Joy-Giver! But I believe the Bible teaches that the more joy we give the more we receive. The gift God has given to us should be felt in our hearts, seen in our lives, shared with others, and should not be hidden under a bushel . . . as the song goes.

"*Let your life shine before men in such a way that they may see your good works, and glorify your Father who is in heaven.*" (Matthew 5:16)

A smile is a bud flowering into laughter the moment it feels the sunshine of God's mercy and grace. Joy is a plant, watered by God's Word, and, because it grows in the rich soil of God's love, it releases a sweet fragrance that others are drawn to.

George Eliot, a Christian giant, has been quoted as saying, "Wear a smile and have friends; wear a scowl and have wrinkles." I can think of few benefits attributed to scowling, but a myriad of blessings emanate from a smile. Choose a smile or a hearty laugh, and it is like getting a shot in the arm, without the jag.

Some of the most memorable moments are when my wit-gifted children come home for holiday celebrations. It can begin with just one little word, or a short sentence, but it inevitably ends in stomach-wrenching laughter, as one picks up on the words of the other, until it builds to a crescendo of endless mirth. Many times I have had to excuse myself from the dinner table, feeling like I had just dashed around the world—so much energy expended on laughter. Laughter is one of those priceless gifts from God.

One Christmas, I came up with what I thought was a terrific idea for gifts for my four children.

After my mother died, I became the proud owner of her ancient two-ton Sunbeam Mix-Master, known best for its ability to mash potatoes into the most flavorful and cloud-like substance you could ever imagine. There was not a lump to be found in those famous Mix-Master Potatoes. They were the envy of the family and the neighborhood.

Over the ensuing years, my four children sought to come up with a fair and balanced plan for enjoying those same mouth-watering mashed potatoes, after I had gone home to be with the Lord. But the question remained: how do you divide one Sunbeam Mix-Master among four children? Do you give one the beaters, one the head of the mixer, one the bowl and the other the stand? That didn't seem to make much sense to me, since they would have had to gather from different states in the union to enjoy those fluffy lumpless potatoes. I decided that was not a practical or a convenient arrangement.

Based on their obvious dilemma, I finally came up with a plan. I decided to use the six available months before the next Christmas family gathering, to search for four ancient, two-ton, Sunbeam Mix-Masters. You must understand, a new Sunbeam Mixer would never have cut it with my children. It had to be a mixer like Grandma used and was now being used by their mother.

Much to my surprise and delight, I managed to locate four of the exact same Sunbeam Mix-Masters, just like my mother and I had enjoyed for many years. As an antique dealer myself, I am familiar with all the hiding places for such treasures!

I was so excited for Christmas to arrive that year! I carefully boxed and wrapped each mixer and topped the packages off with beautiful bows. But then something occurred to me: What if some of my children couldn't be home for Christmas that year? It did happen on occasion, since at least two or three at a time resided outside the state of Pennsylvania, where I lived. Not wanting to take the chance of missing out on the delight in their eyes on Christmas morning, when they would become proud owners of their very own Sunbeam Mix-Masters, I decided to send each one of them a special Christmas invitation. I was very emphatic about the importance of them coming home that particular Christmas, saying that I would not take "no" for an answer.

My invitation must have been convincing enough, because it wasn't long before each of my children responded favorably to attending this very special family Christmas Celebration, the birth of Jesus, in Mt. Gretna, Pennsylvania, that year.

I could barely endure the suspense. I began to imagine all kinds of reactions to their unexpected gifts, not short of all out leaping and shouting with delight! I was absolutely certain they would be overjoyed to have their very own old, two-ton, Sunbeam Mix-Masters, without having to wait until I died! It certainly took the onus off me to hasten my departure!

Christmas finally came, and there beneath the Christmas tree were four very large packages, equal in size and content. The size of the packages wouldn't have come as a surprise to my children, since I often wrapped small gifts in very large packages. The Mix-Master packages stood out among all the other gifts that had been purchased, with equal love and joy, for my grandchildren.

After having a few snacks and a time of thanking God for the birth of His Son Jesus, it was time to open our presents.

I was so excited! But that's an understatement. I was beside myself! In fact, I don't think there was ever a Christmas when I had been so ecstatic. It took every bit of restraint I could muster not to open the gifts myself.

I looked around the living room. I noticed some puzzled looks being exchanged between my four adult children. I chalked the exchanges up to anticipation and bewilderment over what in the world was contained in the four large boxes. Even the grandchildren seemed to be enthralled with the suspense of what was in the personally marked boxes for their mother and uncles.

Not unlike the starting line at an automobile race—waiting for the green flag to mark the start of the race—I instructed my adult children to begin opening their gifts. Noticing their apprehension, apparently still waiting for the flag, I realized they were waiting for me to tell them which one should begin opening their gift first. So, I said, "Oh, you can all open them simultaneously."

I sat there waiting, barely able to contain myself. I was already on the edge of my seat.

My oldest son was the first to reach the treasure inside the beautifully wrapped box, then my next to oldest son retrieved his prize, followed by my youngest son, and last but not least, my daughter pulled her three-part gift from her box. The room grew quiet, as four adult children sat there with the beaters in one hand and the base in the other. Looking at one another, in what I perceived to be a state of shock at this most special of all moments and gifts, the laughter and joy I expected to emerge instantly from my normally witty children, seemed to have gotten lost amidst the wrappings. I thought to myself, *what were they expecting?* It was obvious they weren't expecting Sunbeam Mix-Masters, but neither did they indicate delight in receiving the long sought after and much coveted gifts.

Suddenly, one of them began to laugh, then another, then another, and another, until they were bent over in laughter. It must have been very difficult for them to admit to me, after they had exhausted themselves laughing, the real reason for their unexpected reactions to the gifts.

"Should we tell her?" asked one of my sons, checking with his siblings.

All heads nodded "yes."

They finally confessed to me that, after receiving my very emphatic invitation to come home for Christmas, they had begun communicating with each other over the phone, trying to figure out why urgency seemed to surround their Christmas appearance. Now they were about to reveal their conclusion to me.

"Mother, we finally decided, after talking back and forth over these many months, that you were going to give us our inheritance!"

After a few moments of silence and surprise, I said, "I did give you your inheritance! It's a two-ton Sunbeam Mix Master!"

Ho! Ho! Ho!

Now there's a very good reason to laugh!

How difficult it must have been for them, to find Sunbeam Mix-Masters in their beautifully wrapped packages, instead of an anticipated financial inheritance, and still be able to give thanks and turn that disappointment into hours of joy and laughter, as we made lasting memories together that Christmas.

The eventual breakdown of those old mixers continued to bring laughter years after that momentous holiday. In the end, it was the laughter they remembered sharing, not the disappointment or empty pockets, as they returned home.

Another occasion in promoting laughter in the family was when I engaged a limousine and a dinner reservation at a fine restaurant as a way of elaborately celebrating several of our birthdays.

Once again, my obedient children arrived home in Pennsylvania for another one of their mother's surprise gifts.

The limousine arrived, as hired, and the children and I, all dressed to the nines for that special event, climbed into the spacious, long, black limousine. Unbeknownst to them, I had prearranged for the driver of the limousine to pull into a McDonald's drive-through and order four Happy-Meals! Yes, the same expressions crossed their faces, as we revisited the Sunbeam Mix-Master Christmas.

Before I had a chance to tell them that the Happy Meals were to be eaten by the limousine driver, they began sampling them, thinking that McDonald's was all there was to the night's celebration, and they began laughing. By now, I'm sure they thought their mother had entered the early stages of "most-of-the-timers." They were soon relieved to find that a lovely pre-decorated birthday table awaited them at an elegant local restaurant.

During the festivities of the evening, many people came to our table and said they had never heard such joy and laughter shared among a family of siblings and their mother. The rewards of joy are everlasting, and people really do want "some of dat!"

Conversely, I find that I cry using equal amounts of energy when a tragedy enters my life. I believe Oswald Chambers said it best: "Laughter and weeping are the two intensest forms of human emotion, and these profound wells of human emotion are to be consecrated to God."

God, most certainly made it possible for us to enjoy the freedom to laugh and to cry. If God collects the tears of His children in a bottle, I am convinced that a bouquet of laughter will grace the banquet table of Heaven one day: *"You have taken account of my wanderings; put my tears in Your bottle." (Psalm 56:8, 9)*

If you are redeeming your time on "Mt. Misery" (the name of an actual retreat location), you need a mudslide that brings you to your knees before the Lord, in gratitude for His mercy and grace and for the sacrifice He made so that you can have life and joy and have it abundantly.

Joys recorded in Scripture are too numerous to include them all in this small already joy-full book, but they are there for you to find, read, and apply to your life, so that your joy might be full. What's felt in your heart will radiate on your face, if you believe you are free to laugh.

"*It was for freedom that Christ set us free . . .* " *(Galatians 5:1)* We have been set free to laugh, to choose right from wrong and to choose joy. The Scriptures seem to ask this question: "If you were under bondage at one time, bondage under the elemental things of the world, who set you free?" The answer is found in *Galatians 4:4* "*. . . when the fullness of the time came, God sent forth His Son . . .* " That is who set you free from bondage. We who believe have become sons of God. *"Therefore you are no longer a slave, but a son; and if a son, then an heir through God." (Galatians 4:7)*

Liberty and freedom are found in Jesus. Are you smiling? If not, why not? Are you a son or daughter of the Heavenly Father? If you aren't, what's keeping you from becoming a member of the family of God, through trust in Jesus?

If you are a believer, and your life lacks luster, there is something else for you to consider. As Billy Sunday, a great evangelist once said, "If you have no joy in your religion, there's a leak in your Christianity somewhere."

Freedom and liberty are yours, it's already been paid for; all you must do is accept it through faith in Jesus.

CHAPTER TWO

Did Jesus Laugh?

✻ Laurette Connelly ✻

My ministry partner, Veda, and I have a Christian speaking ministry in which we often incorporate nonsensical skits that will sometimes bring the house down with side-splitting laughter. We both feel that Jesus has opened the door for this ministry and filled our mouths with fun and humor. Hopefully, the sound of laughter reaches up to the highest heaven to make even Jesus laugh at the whimsical behavior of His less than stoic children.

"*Our mouths were filled with laughter, our tongues with songs of joy. Then it was said among the nations, 'The Lord has done great things for them.' The Lord has done great things for us, and we are filled with joy.*" (Psalm 126:2-3)

We all have moments in our lives that make us turn beet red at the thought of them. Like the time I followed a "Garage Sale" sign to the top of a hill in a lush residential neighborhood. Spotting a littered driveway, I quickly made my way to a beautiful Schwinn ten-speed bike. I first lowered the seat till it was the right height for me, then climbed aboard and cruised around the cul-de-sac a few times before a gentleman asked if he could help me. "No," I said, "I'm just browsing." Setting the bicycle aside I opened up a practically new lawn chair and stretched myself out comfortably to be sure it was a good fit. Again the man said, "Excuse me, are you looking for something?" *He sure is a pest,* I thought to myself as I opened up the lid to an outdoor grill. "You don't have anything priced," I said. "I might be interested in that bike." When he looked at me like I had spaghetti coming out of my ears, I knew something was not right with this picture. "Lady," he said, "I'm cleaning my garage."

Not knowing where to look at that point all I could think of was to say something totally off the wall. "Does that mean you won't sell me the bike?"

Fortunately, the man had a sense of humor. He burst out laughing and called his wife, Tillie, to meet this goofy woman. We all had a good laugh together. I assume they were laughing with me and not at me, but I'll never be sure. Like me, he's probably still telling the story and getting a chuckle over it twenty years later.

Laughter is part of living, it's one of the things that distinguish us from other created beings on this earth. To deny ourselves the release of laughter is to rob ourselves of one of the healthiest gifts given to man. Without laughter our insides can begin to age and shrivel up before their time.

Jesus, being fully man, would have to laugh at some of the things that happen in life. He was the oldest of several children, surely the antics of younger siblings would have made Him laugh "with them" at times. Who can resist laughing with a one year old who is just learning to eat by himself, to walk and talk? God chose to keep Jesus' childhood private, but we know that He grew up in a loving home. We can imagine that as a child He might have played games with His younger brothers and sisters, at times.

Marbles and throwing games with leather balls were popular in Jesus' day. That kind of play would have brought giggles and laughter. When He apprenticed in the carpentry shop with His foster father Joseph, and friends and neighbors dropped in to have chairs, benches, carts, wagon wheels, and children's toys repaired, did they not have conversations that would have sometimes brought a smile, a grin or even a guffaw of laughter?

"Isn't this the carpenter? Isn't this Mary's son and the brother of James, Joseph, Judas and Simon? Aren't his sisters here with us?" (Mark 6:3)

Is it possible that a man would attend a wedding with his family and friends but never laugh? A marriage ceremony then, as now, was a time of rejoicing. Friends would go in torchlight procession to the home prepared for the newly married couple. Often they were accompanied with music and dancing. Everyone would be expected to rejoice with the bride and groom. I suppose that, along with the other guests, Jesus would have joined in the celebration and His loving countenance would have reflected joy, and accordingly, laughter.

Could a man spend three years in very close contact with a group of men He called friends and never allow them to see Him laugh? I don't think so. Jesus was, of course, one hundred percent God so He could do anything. But He was also one hundred percent man (except without sin) and in relating to mankind He would have allowed Himself to express many emotions, especially through laughter. Those occasions when they sat before a campfire or reclined at a host's table, just He and the twelve, there had to be times of laughter and even hilarity as they shared stories about their experiences, their work and their families.

Recently, I had the pleasure of spending a week at the shore in North Carolina with sixteen ladies ranging in age from fifty-five to eighty. We all live in the same community but until that week, most of us were simply acquaintances and a couple were virtually strangers to many because they were new to our neighborhood.

Lasting friendships were cemented during that therapeutic week, which I count as a gift from the Lord. Serious conversations took place during long walks on the beach or on secluded porches here and there as those who came with anxieties and heavy burdens felt the freedom to share with others who offered a listening ear or even a padded shoulder.

One of the ladies had just completed a long series of chemotherapy treatments. One evening as we circled around the table for "pizza" night, she gallantly whipped off her temporary wig and announced, "This is just too hot and I think we all know each other well enough by now that I can feel free to take this ugly, bothersome thing off." Her reply came in the form of a rousing round of applause and cheers for this dear lady who had won our admiration with her courageous spirit.

There was time for ministry as women from all backgrounds gathered for a Sunday morning ecumenical worship service, praising the Lord for a time of rest and fun while ultimately knitting our lives together.

The most valuable friendship-building times of all were evenings when we all sat around in the living room after a day in the sun to just talk and get to know each other. Invariably, someone ended up rolling on the floor in uncontrollable laughter as one woman after another dug into her treasury of embarrassing moments or told of an outlandish experience she'd had. A close camaraderie sown in tears and laughter brought about strong ties that I can hardly imagine will ever be severed.

Jesus and the twelve must have had similar experiences. They not only spent three years in very close contact but they also worked closely together long after Jesus was crucified. Could every moment of their time together have been weighty teaching and studying, trying to absorb great truths and to retain it all? Jesus knew the importance and benefits of taking time off from the pressures of the world.

When the apostles returned from their first missionary journey they were excited and exhausted from having ministered to the needy. What's more, they were met with the heartache of the news that their friend, John the Baptist, had been beheaded. Tensions were high and hearts were heavy.

Vance Havner has said, "If you don't come apart and rest, you'll just come apart." Even Jesus needed time to rest and fellowship with His friends. *"And He said to them, 'Come aside by yourselves to a deserted place and rest awhile.' So they went away by themselves in a boat to a solitary place." (Mark 6:31, 32)*

That solitary place could have been on the beach or some quiet place where they had restorative time. I can hardly conceive that a time of unwinding would not include laughter. Even in the midst of pitiful circumstances and difficult ministry there's generally some type of comic relief.

Peter with his impetuous temperament must have had an invaluable storehouse of embarrassing moments, which would have brought even the most serious of persons to hysterics. A strong alliance between them could only be formed by a sincere revelation of individual personalities. Yes, I believe there were times when the apostles were caught up in hilarious laughter that left them weak. Behind closed doors there had to be times of teary-eyed laughter with Christ at the center laughing right along with them, encouraging the relief and release of tension from the daily grind of heavy-duty ministry.

For several years I was involved in the Evangelism Explosion ministry at my church in New Jersey. As a teacher trainer I was out with two trainees one evening. We were assigned to visit a large apartment building in the inner city. It was a rainy Monday night. The building was a run-down tenement where the plaster in the halls was cracked and falling down, and stair rails were loose with missing spindles. Entering the building our nostrils were overcome with a smorgasbord of aromas. Sounds varied from parents arguing, children crying, and televisions blaring. As we knocked on door after door we found most had several locks and bolts on them and the occupants were most reticent to open their door to any outsider.

One very young woman, on the first floor opened her door only a couple of inches leaving the bolt on. She had a small sobbing child in her arms and another clinging to her skirt for security. Her pretty young face had clearly been marred from a recent beating. "I can't talk to you," she said in a fearful, trembling voice just above a whisper. "Please go away or I'll be in serious trouble." We gave her a tract and asked if we could help in any way. "No," she said, "just go away, I don't want your help, I don't want anyone's help. I'm okay."

With heavy hearts and a gamut of emotions, we had no choice but to leave this frightened young mom with seemingly no place to turn for help. We continued to cover the first floor but no doors would open to us. We heard only muffled sounds telling us to "Go away." "No solicitors," one person shouted in a loud, angry voice. Reaching the second floor we met a man named Charlie who was very glad for the company. He not only let us into his home, but Charlie proceeded to show us faded family photos going back three generations. Charlie was an older man with a graying beard and a few missing teeth. He went on to explain that he was single again after raising eight children. Charlie loved to tell jokes and would have gladly gone through his entire repertoire if we hadn't put an end to it. He was preparing to audition for a small part in a local theatre musical production. It was his first tryout in many years and he was most eager for an audience. Charlie insisted on reading his lines to us so we could provide a no cost critiquing service for his yet undiscovered talent.

Popping a smelly, chewed-up old cigar in his mouth, he pretended to come in the door and slam it behind him. "Mabel, I'm home! Where are you, woman?" he yelled. "Did you pick up a six-pack for me today? I'm bushed! Hey, where's my girlie magazines? You better not have thrown them out, Mabel, or you're goin' on a one-way trip to the moon!"

"What do you think? Did that sound like a tough guy who's had a few beers on his way home from work? That's what my character is supposed to be doing. So what do you think?" he asked. Charlie fancied himself to be an overlooked but talented thespian. He expected his captive audience to give him rave reviews for his award winning, though impromptu and unrequested performance.

After twenty minutes of listening and trying to break through to Charlie, we decided that he wasn't about to listen to anything we had to say. We gave him a quick round of quiet applause, left tracts and excused ourselves, wishing him the best in his local debut.

With the third floor came the prize we'd been working for all evening. As we stood outside this apartment door the sound of the television was blaring with the noise of Monday night football and the loud cheering of enthusiastic fans.

"We'll never get in there!" the two young trainees exclaimed with agreed discouragement. Undaunted, I knocked on the door. A burly young man clad only in his plaid undershorts, opened the door and said, "Yeah?" When I told him who we were and what we were doing, he said, "Wait a minute," and closed the door. I thought I would never see him again but a minute or two later, he came back with his trousers on. He ushered us into a one-room apartment devoid of furniture, except for a mattress on the floor, a small refrigerator, a tiny table and a couple of straight back chairs. Two other young men, probably in their mid-thirties, sat on the floor glued to the television. They were completely absorbed in what was obviously an exciting game. Probably because they would have considered our visit a very unwelcome intrusion, neither one ever looked up or acknowledged our presence.

The young man who had let us in introduced himself as Richard. He gave me one of the chairs and another to one of the trainees. The second trainee sat on the floor while Richard took his position on the bare mattress.

"Is there someplace quiet we could go to talk?" I asked, hoping there might be another room attached to this one somewhere.

"Lady, it's either this or the bathroom," said Richard.

"Oh, well, then this will be fine," I said. "We can talk here."

"Okay, talk," said Richard with what struck me as a challenging tone, almost daring me to say something that could possibly spark even an ounce of interest in him.

Over the noise of one fumble and two touchdowns by the Philadelphia Eagles and Baltimore Colts, I was able to present the Gospel to Richard.

Halfway through, Richard interrupted me and asked, "You mean Jesus will take all my sins and He's willing to forgive me for every one of them from day one?"

"Yes," I said, "That's what God tells us. He died for all and God has laid on Him the iniquity of us all. It's not His desire that any should perish."

With that, Richard reached down beside the stripped down mattress and pulled up a new paraphrased Bible. "Can you show me where it says that in the Bible?" he asked.

I read to him from 2 Peter 3:9 and several other passages. I could almost hear the silent prayers of the two trainees as they offered Godly support.

"*The Lord is not slack concerning His promise, as some count slackness, but is longsuffering toward us, not willing that any should perish but that all should come to repentance.*" (2 Peter 3:9)

"*Come now, let us reason together,*" *says the Lord.* "*Though your sins are like scarlet, they shall be as white as snow; though they are red as crimson, they shall be like wool.*" (Isaiah 1:18)

"*In My Father's house are many mansions; if it were not so, I would have told you. I go to prepare a place for you. And if I go and prepare a place for you, I will come again and receive you to Myself; that where I am, there you may be also.*" (John 14:2)

"*We all, like sheep, have gone astray, each of us has turned to his own way; and the LORD has laid on him the iniquity of us all.*" (Isaiah 53:6)

Richard was noticeably hanging on to every word, stopping me now and then to ask an earnest question. When I finished giving the Gospel presentation, this huge man who had intimidated me at the beginning, had now become a gentle giant dissolved into very heart-gripping, poignant tears.

The two young trainees sat in awe, visibly moved at what they knew was happening in that dreary room. The darkness was being dispelled by the Spirit of God doing a mighty work of awakening in young men's lives.

"Richard, after what you've heard, would you like to receive Jesus as your Lord and Savior?" I asked.

"I've wanted that all my life," he cried. "I can't believe you came here tonight. I can't tell you how long I've been trying to figure this out for myself. I've gone to church for years and I had bits and pieces but it never came together before."

"We really need to find a quiet corner somewhere where we can pray with you," I said.

Just then, one of the other young men who still had never looked up or showed any recognition that anyone was even in the same room with them, got up and turned the television off. When I looked up at him, I saw a steady stream of tears cascading from his piercing blue eyes.

"You heard every word we said, didn't you?" I said practically in tears myself at this point. "What's your name?"

"Tony, my name is Tony. I'm a cop in town and I see people hurting and dying all the time. They're always so scared. I see it on their faces and I can't help them. I don't know how to help them," he said. "What you said to my buddy, do you think I could have that too, would that include me? God knows I've never been an angel, I've done some things I'm not proud of, but if God can forgive Richard, maybe He can forgive me too."

Unmistakably, we three; the trainees, John and Andrew, and myself, had been sent on a divine appointment. I was sure they must have been hearing the beating of my heart at the excitement of seeing these two street-wise young men seeking the God of all comfort. Thanking God for the privilege of being sent I looked at the third person in that room who had still made no attempt toward admitting that we were there and I popped up an urgent prayer. "Lord, there are three young men here and I'm not leaving 'til we speak to the third."

"What's your name?" I dared to ask him. "Did you hear what we've been talking about?"

He not only had heard but he too was ready. Ryan was his name and he was in the process of fighting a messy divorce that he definitely didn't want, but he seemed to believe there was no other solution, no way out.

"*There hath no temptation taken you but such as is common to man: but God is faithful, who will not suffer you to be tempted above that ye are able; but will with the temptation also make a way to escape, that ye may be able to bear it.*" (1 Corinthians 10:13)

Before we left that apartment, all three young men sat and prayed to receive Jesus as their Lord and Savior. They were excited and asking questions about where they could get more information and who would give them guidance. We made arrangements for someone to call on them the following week. After sharing a weepy group hug we left them behind and let the Spirit of God take over.

As the team walked down the dilapidated staircase I was totally spent, my legs felt like they would go out from under me at any time. I knew that power had left me and was now in the upstairs room where three young men had been ushered into the eternal kingdom by the Spirit of Almighty God. It was the most exuberant and exhausting appointment I ever had in five years of evangelistic visits.

It's now twelve years later and I am still emotional when I think of those three men waiting for someone to knock on their door to bring them the good news. God could have sent anyone. It didn't have to be me. But I'm so grateful that He chose me for the job. I can't help but wonder how their lives might have changed over the years. Is that policeman still on the force and is he now able to bring words of hope to dying people? I wonder if Ryan and his wife have reconciled and are they walking with the Lord?

Unquestionably, the apostles had comparable experiences that left them entirely spent and exhausted after meeting with their own Richards. But the Charlies in their lives would have brought a chuckle or two mixed with heartfelt concern for their salvation.

Jesus had many disciples and followers besides the twelve. During His short life, He developed strong friendships on this earth. Counted among special friends were Lazarus and his two sisters, Mary and Martha who lived in the quiet little village of Bethany. It was to Martha that Jesus first declared, *"I am the resurrection and the life. He who believes in me will live, even though he dies."*

It was a short walk from the temple at Jerusalem and when Jesus the Messiah was passing through town, He felt the freedom to drop in on His friends. Probably He would have been unannounced and accompanied by a few of His disciples. When Martha greeted Him warmly and invited them in for a meal, Jesus must have smiled, or even laughed at her excitement to see Him as He graciously accepted her invitation. The family had a close and intimate relationship with Jesus. Over the years they must have shared special times of laughter. When Lazarus died they also shared heartache and sorrow.

"When Jesus saw her weeping, and the Jews who had come along with her also weeping, He was deeply moved in spirit and troubled. 'Where have you laid him?' He asked. 'Come and see, Lord,' they replied. Jesus wept." (John 11:33-35)

John's Gospel was written to show us the deity of Christ. Here Jesus is shown in all His humanness. Clearly Jesus displayed human emotions, His spirit was troubled and He wept. His compassion was not for Lazarus but for all those who were dissolved into tears all around him. His compassion also came from a deep sense of the pain that sin had brought into the world. He also knew that while Lazarus would be raised again to this world, yet he would one day have to face the pain of death all over again.

Later the Messiah also celebrated with these same friends at a special dinner given in His honor. They were having a party for Him maybe to express gratitude for raising Lazarus from the dead. Again, in that sort of happy atmosphere, there must have been laughter even though Jesus knew He was walking in the shadow of that ugly cross.

"Six days before the Passover, Jesus arrived at Bethany, where Lazarus lived, whom Jesus had raised from the dead. Here a dinner was given in Jesus' honor. Martha served, while Lazarus was among those reclining at the table with him. Then Mary took a pound of very costly oil of spikenard, anointed the feet of Jesus, and wiped His feet with her hair. And the house was filled with the fragrance of the oil." (John 12:1-3)

The word 'joy' or 'rejoice' is mentioned ten times in the book of John alone and seventy-seven times in the New Testament. That indicates to me that joy is important to God. Jesus had the joy of our salvation. That joy had to bring a happy smile to His glorious face. It was His dying wish that we should be 'filled' with joy.

"I am coming to you now, but I say these things while I am still in the world, so that they may have the full measure of my joy within them." (John 17:13)

He encouraged his disciples to have happy hearts: *"These things I have spoken to you, that in Me you may have peace. In the world you will have tribulation; but be of good cheer, I have overcome the world." (John 16:33)*

Yes, I am personally convinced that our joyful, wonderful, loving Savior not only smiled but that He had times of hearty laughter with the people He loved enough to come and rescue them from the pit of hell.

CHAPTER THREE

Benefits of Laughter

🐝 *Veda Boyd* 🐝

"Open your mouth and say HA!"
- Veda Boyd

Disciplining myself to jog five miles a day did not come from a deep desire to win some silver-plated trophy or a twenty-six-mile marathon. Most of the time I am hot and looking like a red beet, just trying to complete the last mile standing up. I repeated that routine, year after year, not because of the joy it brought into my life, but because I knew how good I felt after I completed the run and how good it was for my physical and psychological well being.

The medical profession now promotes laughter as good medicine, an exercise that can have tremendous healing power, and that prayer can help get you through some of the most difficult times.

Not everyone pre-medicates with laughter and prayer before visiting the dentist or facing surgery, but doing so could very well mean the difference between *helplessness* and *hopefulness*. Too often, we choose to overdose on "what ifs" and indulge in an uninterrupted regimen of "worry," and stress-paralysis sets in. If only we would believe and trust more. Instead, we lose our grip on God, grit our teeth and head for the exit sign.

As a white-knuckle flyer, I am not a stranger to exit signs. I look for them in hotels, in restaurants, in hospitals, and particularly in airplanes. The escape route in air has its drawbacks however. I read somewhere that there are fifty ways to leave our lover, but there are only four ways out of an airplane. Knowing my history, I would probably choose the wrong way.

Recently, "Odds and Ends" was invited to speak in Iowa. Now, let me remind you, I live in Pennsylvania. If we accepted the invitation (which we did), we would either have to drive or fly to Iowa. Walking was ruled out as a method of transportation, much to my chagrin.

With my overwhelming fear of flying (and that's putting it mildly), I first suggested to my partner "Ret" that we drive to Iowa. After much consideration, we realized that driving would not be practical, since I had a work schedule to consider. At that moment, I was seriously considering taking Superman to Iowa, until I learned he doesn't fly there anymore.

With a host of prayer partners behind me and a pocket full of Bible verses, I made it to the airport. Believe me, it took all that to get me there.

When we entered the international airport grounds, I saw a sign that read: "AIRPORT LEFT." I immediately grasped at straws and the reverse gear on my CRV Honda. "Ret," I said, "we may as well turn around and go home, that sign says the airport isn't here anymore; it's left!" She looked at me, and in her eyes I read her thoughts, the ones she was kind enough not to verbalize. *And I picked you for a speaking partner!*

We did eventually get on the airplane—a very small commuter jet with the name "American Eagle" painted on the side. It didn't take me long to figure out how it earned that name. It looked to be no larger than an American eagle, the kind that perches on a tree, which I was hoping this eagle would not do. I sauntered down the aisle sideways, not by choice, but because it was too narrow to do otherwise, to the last two seats in the tail section of the airplane – just where I always wanted to be! I know very little about airplanes, but from speaking to pilot friends and my flight attendant son, that is not the most ideal seat for an infrequent fearful flyer. My friend looked at me and said, with a smile, "It's the safest place if there's a crash." She seemed actually pleased with her words of reassurance. Now, usually this lady cracks me up, but somehow, I didn't find her comment comforting, or the least bit humorous. I responded with one of those disingenuous grins—the ones that could kill if they could speak.

The airplane was one I wouldn't have wished for in my wildest dreams or even as a balsa-wood model in my Christmas stocking as a kid, and my fears began to multiply.

Our first stop was in Chicago, where we boarded yet another commuter jet to our final destination. Ditto! Another American Eagle. I am now convinced that, when I go to heaven, I will first have to stop in Chicago and I'll get an American Eagle instead of a chariot of gold.

Little did I anticipate that the final leg of our trip would produce some spectacular evidence of God's sovereignty, His love for me (and for you), and His faithful presence with us through our trials, even in the "not so friendly skies" between Chicago and Iowa.

After what happened to me, I couldn't help thinking about the young man on the hijacked plane that went down in Pennsylvania on 9/11 and the certainty he must have felt that God was with him even as he faced certain death. I believe angels circled the plane that fell in Pennsylvania that day, and He ushered those who were His children into the presence of His glory and they were met with the joyful songs and sounds of heaven.

As I sat frozen in the seat of that small commuter jet with one flight attendant and thirty-five minutes to Iowa from Chicago—I neither spoke, smiled, or even thought about the treats we were informed "we wouldn't get" due to the short leg of our flight. And that's saying something because I usually think a lot about food!

It wasn't long before the flight attendant, an attractive young African American girl, approached our row of seats. She took one look at me and asked, "Do you have a question?"

No, I thought to myself, *I have an acute case of fear*.

Again, she tried to get a response from me.

"Do you have a question; are you all right?"

At that point, when my friend Ret determined I was too frightened to speak, she decided she would speak for me.

"No, she is not OK; she is petrified of flying."

With that obvious revelation, besides the drips of blood coming from my clenched fingers and white knuckles, the flight attendant announced that she would be right back. When she returned, she asked, "Do you know Jesus?"

I replied, "Yes, of course I do."

"Sweetie," she said, "God did not give us a spirit of fear. The Bible says that perfect love casts out fear, and so I'm going to lay my hands on you and I'm going to ask Jesus to remove the fear you have right now."

Before I had a chance to consider her boldness, I felt her warm obedient hand upon my shoulder, and I listened to her pray. When she was finished, I felt a portion of fear leave my body, enough that I could reasonably relax and allow my mind to undergo the change needed to remind me of the faith and trust I have in Jesus Christ, and that He is with us ALWAYS!

"... *I am with you always, even to the end of the age.*" *(Matthew 28:20)*

God had just sent an angel to minister to me, and her name was Laverne. I am thankful that His angel was obedient and was willing to carry out her mission. She told us how being a flight attendant was not just a job for her, but it was her mission and ministry, one she would obey by sharing God's love, and the comfort He provides, with anyone on her flight that she felt God was leading her to. She had picked me out immediately and I knew that God chose her to minister to me that day. Praise God that she was faithful and bold enough to fulfill the mission God had given her to complete on that flight to Iowa.

When we exited the plane in Iowa, she handed both Ret and me a little card. I carry it with me at all times. It reads: *"Lord, remind me that nothing is going to happen today that You and I together can't handle!"* And on the back of the card, she hand wrote these words: *"Just a reminder—The Greater one lives inside of you. It's a pleasure to know you. God bless you and your loved ones, Laverne."*

If I had not taken that flight to Iowa, with a stopover in Chicago, I would not have had the privilege of meeting one of God's angels, one that was up to the job, on the job! THANK GOD FOR

LAVERNE AND HER FAITHFULNESS TO SERVE HIM IN SUCH A SPECIAL WAY! I also thanked my friend "Ret" for her patience and prayers while suffering along with me. Only a true friend could endure such a load. I believe Laverne, the angel, was also for Ret's benefit—to bolster her faith and trust as well—even though she is a much more courageous flyer than I will ever be.

It was later determined, by Ret's son, the pastor of the church in which we were scheduled to speak, that I am not afraid to fly or to die, I'm just afraid to "fall." That made a lot of sense to me. I'm going to charter a low flying saucer to our next speaking engagement. What insight!

A spirit of calmness in the midst of trials can be ours, from a God who understands our circumstances, because He was tempted in all ways as we are. *"Cast all your anxiety on Him, because He cares for you." (I Peter 5:7)*

Jesus was able to endure the pain of the cross because His hope and trust were in His Heavenly Father—exactly where ours should be. You might be saying, "Well, the Bible says Jesus wept and pleaded with His Father to take the cup of death from Him." Indeed, you say right, but He followed that plea with these words: *"Not my will Father, but yours." (Luke 22:42)* How often do we administer those words as a soothing ointment when we face serious illness or possible deadly circumstances? Do the steady hands of God comfort us when ours are shaking?

I admit my own lack of faith when it comes to flying, and I thought it's high–time (pun intended) that I swallowed my own medicine and practiced what I speak about. Although, I still contend that God said, *"Lo, I am with you always,"* not high I am with you always! But I won't leave you hanging there. I know for sure, and I believe these words that are recorded in the Bible: *"For I am convinced that neither death, nor life, nor angels, nor principalities, nor things present, nor things to come, nor powers, nor height, nor depth, nor any other created thing, will be able to separate us from the love of God, which is in Christ Jesus our Lord." (Romans 8:38, 39)* Of course, God doesn't stop there. The Bible says, *"And who of you by being worried can add a single hour to his life?" (Matthew 6:27)*

It has been suggested that my fear of flying is a "control thing, and even perhaps a lack of trust." Maybe that is also true of you and why you lack the joy and peace that can be yours through confidence in Christ. I know that that's probably as close as I'll ever get to understanding my fear of flying. It's so hard to give up the pilot's seat, isn't it? I mean, I used to take a motorcycle around corners that would make any man cry, and take "S-turns" wide and on the inside in my sports car, but I was behind the wheel and the handlebars; I was in control—or so I thought. It takes a whole lot of trust to give up control to someone else, and yet, that is what God requires of us; it is exactly that kind of surrender that produces joy. It's a little like saying we love the Lord, yet we continually sin against Him and others. If we say we have faith and yet persist in living with fear and distrust, we are guilty of "faith contradiction." That is not to say that, if I fall into a lion's den, I have nothing to fear. To the contrary, I best try and get out of there fast! It is not ungodly to possess healthy consternation in certain circumstances, but to remain there, immensely reduces our joy experience. Trust and true joy are synonymous and they most certainly produce health benefits, just as laughter does. It was true of my flight to Iowa. Trust and faith in the sovereign God was what gave me the courage to look out of the airplane window. Jesus wants us to put ourselves under His care completely. But if you are thinking that's an excuse not to go to work tomorrow and just allow God to take care of you, it won't work. He tells us to observe the ant—how the ant works—but not to be caught up in working so hard and so long that we miss the benefit of being in His presence.

Diagnosed with cancer years ago, and lying beneath what looked more like a huge flying saucer than an operating-room light, a host of aliens dressed in white surrounded the operating table. I recall looking up into their masked faces and saying, "OK, beam me up Scottie!" The last thing I heard, or remembered after that, was laughter; imagine laughter over the operating table!

Since that time, I have concluded that, trust and attitude are probably half the physical and mental battle when facing difficult circumstances. I have not always felt that way. But the more I learn about our Lord, the more I realize that He is able, more than able, to see us through difficult times and 35,000 foot heights. *"Now to Him who is able to do far more abundantly beyond all that we ask or think, according to the power that works with us." (Ephesians 3:20)*

Jesus said that He would give us the Comforter, the Holy Spirit, and that He would reside in each believer. Then why don't we draw on the Holy Spirit for our comfort? As I so often do, and maybe you do this too—I go it alone, or I wait for God to send me a convincing angel. If you are a believer in Jesus, you are armed with the most powerful weapon against uncertainty and fear. You and I have the power of the Holy Spirit within us, but if you are anything like me, you act and live as if you were powerless. Shame on us!

Lest something not intended be read into what I've just written—let me say this: there are circumstances, such as death, disease, and loss of a front tooth, that are devastating and nearly impossible to endure. Grieving is natural, and Jesus grieved too. *"Jesus wept." (John 11:35)* There is a time to grieve, just as there is a time to laugh. It is those believers who can't tell the difference that concern me.

Not long ago, I had occasion to be in a room full of cheerless Christians. How did I know they were cheerless? They weren't smiling—no not one. To be honest with you, they looked downright "ghostly." The puzzling thing was—they were singing about the joy of the Lord. Had I lingered beyond my allotted fifteen-minute appearance, I myself would have succumbed to that same down-in-the-mouth demeanor. I couldn't help peering into my purse to see if I had a bottle of joy tablets to pass around, but I didn't want to stay that long. There was nothing to attract me to them, or to the Christ in whom they obviously believed. I spent the night in prayer for those downcast worshipers. I truly do not believe it was because they had all lost a loved one that day.

In writing this chapter, I thought it wise to research what some physicians claim regarding the benefits of laughter. I was quite surprised to find pages and pages of evidence to back up what a number of sources, including the Bible, have already suggested: Laughter is good medicine.

Proverbs 17:22 says, *"A merry heart does good like a medicine; but a broken spirit dries up the bones."*

Briefly, the old saying that laughter is the best medicine definitely appears to be true when it comes to protecting your heart, according to my sources. (Detailed information sources listed on "Notes" page of this book.)

An interesting quotation from one of my sources claims that "every organ is being massaged, including your heart, lungs and digestive system when you laugh."

So why would you not want to laugh?

If it has been proven that exercise prolongs life and provides a healthier you, why wouldn't you want to exercise?

If you've ever seen the movie, "Patch Adams," a true story about a medical student who believed laughter had great medicinal value, you will understand the practical benefits of laughter that I have addressed in this chapter. Patch Adams tried desperately to incorporate laughter in his treatment of patients, to the condemnation of many of his colleagues, yet the results of his practical philosophy were seen in the happy faces of those whom he treated.

Our perspective, in the midst of our circumstances is often how our friends, associates, and family diagnose our spiritual condition. Does your demeanor emanate hope or defeat? Have you experienced the benefits of laughter?

If you can't laugh at someone else, or with someone else, then laugh at yourself. Sure, people will think you've lost a few buttons, but that's what they think about me when I'm driving and singing along to a CD in the car—so what?

If you are like me, you do a lot of stupid things, like putting a fresh pack of chicken in the bathroom cupboard only to discover days later, with certainty, that a decomposed body has found its way into your house. It's OK to laugh at yourself.

I do know from experience that one person's laughter can start a room full of people laughing. Recently, my best friend and I went to a restaurant for a hot-fudge sundae. (What else would I go for?) My friend said something funny and I broke out in hysterical laughter. It wasn't long before at least a quarter of the diners had tears rolling down their cheeks from laughing as well. They did not know what we were laughing about—they hadn't heard us talking, but they sure heard us laughing and it wasn't long before they joined in. Many people in that restaurant that night received the benefits of laughter.

Recently, my speaking partner and I were invited to speak at a women's luncheon. Attached was a special request: "Could you please include a lot of humor? There are so many tragedies today; we need to laugh." It was evident to me, by their request, people recognize that laughter heals, renews hope and is a welcome break from the distressing newspaper and television headlines of today. If your mind is fixed on those things, you are being robbed of your joy. *"Whatever is true, whatever is honorable, whatever is right, whatever is pure, whatever is lovely, whatever is of good repute, if there is any excellence and if anything worthy of praise, dwell on these things."* (Philippians 4:8)

After all the articles I have researched, and all the Scripture verses I have read, I am convinced that laughter is good medicine. It's cheap, and you don't need some extended prescription drug program to get a three month's supply of it. I am not claiming that laughter will ever replace organ transplants or circumvent the need for surgery, but I do believe patients can benefit greatly when surrounded by joyful people who are not afraid to smile in the presence of difficult circumstances.

A hearty laugh is better than a good sneeze, though both are reported to create a feeling of euphoria; then why do we suppress them? There are benefits to both: One cleans out your senses and the other cleans out your nose!

When I had open-heart surgery, I was given a cuddly teddy bear to hug when I had to cough, to help ease the physical discomfort resulting from all the invasive procedures. I never had a teddy bear as a child growing up, so I took every advantage of that second childhood moment, which gave me reason to laugh. But it wasn't the furry animal that soothed my heart during that dangerous and delicate time, it was the inner joy I experienced from God's love for me and confidence in His plan for my life.

In my extensive source search for the health benefits of laughter, I read "laughter reduces stress, boosts immunity, relieves pain, decreases anxiety, stabilizes mood, rests the brain, enhances communication, inspires creativity, maintains hope, and bolsters morale." WOW! As the popular Christian singer Carman said in one of his songs, "I want some of dat!"

Not all things are funny, as I mentioned early in this chapter. We cannot ignore that fact. We must practice respect and sensitivity in areas where there are hurting hearts and lost souls, so don't go to the closest funeral home or critical care unit of a hospital and do standup comedy. It won't work, and it shouldn't work. We are instructed to laugh with those who laugh and cry with those who cry. A friend is one who practices that kind of balanced response.

I think of the story of Job in the Bible. My, what trials he faced. Job was a man of integrity and great wealth. Job became the recipient of severe testing of his faith. At his lowest moment, enter Job's friends. Instead of comforting Job, they begin to debate the reasons for his suffering. Of course, they came up empty-handed. God then speaks from a whirlwind, not with condemnation on Job, unlike Job's friends, but to point out His all-powerful ways and Job learns to trust what he cannot understand. That's a difficult assignment at best, at least for me. Job never cursed God through his trails, although his wife suggested he do just that. How different we are, with a whole lot less testing of our faith. We quickly give up on God, on others, and on ourselves, and we are defeated and downcast, and often followed by physical and mental illness. Amazingly, Job prayed for his friends, and God instructed Job's friends to offer up a burnt offering. The Bible says that Job's fortunes were restored when he prayed. It was because of God's goodness and Job's faith and trust that he experienced restoration, physically, mentally and materially. *"His family and friends then surrounded him with comfort, even giving him money and gold rings." (Job 42:11)*

Joy results from a right relationship, not only with God, but also with others, as the account of Job implies. It should be our prayer that we not have to go through trials equal to Job's, but it should also be a clear reminder that we need to speak often of God's love and His power.

Would that I could record on these pages every verse in the Bible that contains the word "rejoice," but I'll leave that for your rich perusal and Bible study time. The freedom to be joyful is ours, and if you aren't smiling you need a faith lift . . . soon.

I know this: my endorphins had a heyday recently while vacationing in the Outer Banks with fifteen other women. Not because the first thing to greet us was a big fat, coiled-up, intimidating snake at the bottom of the steps of our rented property, but from the wonderful attitudes and fun-spirited women who were funny and entertaining without even trying. I would have lost twenty-five pounds from jogging internally and been given a clean bill of health, had it not been for wonderful restaurants and a lengthy drive home that caused some painful blood clots in my left leg. In spite of the discomfort, I'm pleased to report there was humor in the whole incident. Some accused me of developing the blood clots intentionally, to avoid flying to "Odds and Ends" next out-of-state speaking engagement. Boy, I wish I had thought of that! In retrospect, now that you know the outcome of that fearful flight to Iowa, I wouldn't exchange the opportunity for God to show Himself to me anew, in such a miraculous way, high in the air, for any false idea that being on the ground, or even being a Christian, guarantees absolute safety.

One of my sons (and I have three of them), who happens to be a flight attendant for a major airline, told me the story about a frustrating flight he once had. In his attempt to please all several hundred people on the plane, he inadvertently dropped his signature pen on the floor of the plane and was unable to search for it while in flight. When the transatlantic flight finally ended and the plane landed safely, he got down on his knees and tried to retrieve his very costly pen (he has a pen fetish). Seeing him groping around on the floor, one of the passengers asked, "What are you doing? Are you looking for something?" My son replied, "Yes, I'm looking for the glamour in this job, and I can't seem to find it!"

God has given each of my children a terrific sense of humor, and in that case, one of them used it to make people laugh on that airplane, just as God's angel used her gift to bring comfort to my heart during my flight to Iowa.

As one of God's children, you have been given good gifts, and many of you have been gifted with a sense of humor. Unfortunately, many of you haven't yet opened your gift. Then there are those who recognize their gifts but choose not to use them. I can't imagine giving a good gift to someone and never having that person enjoy or even use that gift, but I know it happens. God did not make robots however, so we get to choose how we will use the gifts God gives to us—whether or not they will honor or dishonor Him or rain down joy on others.

The gift of joy we receive from Jesus should be circulated more than any daily newspaper or unsolicited handyman-flyer we find stuck between our door on a regular basis.

When my foster father died, not too many years following my foster mother's death, I discovered drawers stuffed with clothing gifts from friends and family that had never been worn; most still had the store-tags securely fastened. Not only did he miss out on improving his appearance and on the comfort those gifts would have provided, but he disappointed and even hurt the gift givers, including yours truly. I'm sure that God must feel the same way. He generously gives, and we selfishly withhold.

As we recognized the men and women who gave their lives on the one-year anniversary of the tragedy of 9-11-01, I watched the different services in their honor. I thought to myself, *I know if those people were alive today, they would be consumed with joy, overwhelming joy, and thankfulness for the gift of life.* As a survivor of life's experiences and circumstances, what is your response?

If, in the examination of your life, you find yourself laughing at sin, indulging in sin, or accommodating its hold on you, you cannot enjoy the benefits of laughter. If your ears are more in tune with off-color jokes or stories, than to God's Word, you need to be liberated!

Every day I get humorous e-mails. Sometimes I get dozens of them. I find that I must filter and sift out the ones that are not beneficial to me, in order to end up with the ones that lift my spirits and make me laugh. I can tell you, the "Dumb Blonde" jokes are not keepers for me . . . I'm blonde. If we hang out with gloom and doomers, or dwell on the negative events in our lives, there is a good chance we will be sad and unhealthy.

There used to be a popular song in my time (more recent than Bible times), and the words of that song express the exact sentiments I mean to convey regarding "negative parking" (continual dwelling on the negative).

> "Accentuate the positive,
> Eliminate the negative,
> Latch on to the affirmative,
> Don't mess with Mr. In-Between."
> – Harold Arlen and Johnny Mercer

To be characterized by joy is a testament to our relationship with Jesus and to the hope that is in us. If you are struggling to smile today or longing to laugh, you need to latch on to the affirmative. If the process of healing is taking place in your life right now, anticipate joy in the morning. God never intended for His children to be forever sad, forever lonely or forever forsaken. We need to be reminded again that, *"He will never leave or forsake us." (Hebrews 13:5)*

"Let your light shine before men in such a way that they may see your good works, and glorify your Father who is in heaven." (Matthew 5:16)

One of the best ways I can imagine to exercise your joy is to smile. So start now, work those cheek muscles, and reap the benefits of laughter.

CHAPTER FOUR

To Laugh or Not to Laugh

❋ Laurette Connelly ❋

I s it always irreverent to laugh during a church service? Have you ever tried to stifle a laugh that's tickling your insides like you swallowed the entire contents of your feather pillow? Pretty soon you begin to snort, you fake a cough, your shoulders start heaving up and down and you know you are going to lose it. To add to your dilemma the problem seems to be contagious and those sitting beside you quickly catch the bug. They start by snickering but before you know it, their shoulders begin to heave in unison with yours. Trying to retain some semblance of composure and dignity, you grab a tissue and pretend to be broken into tears, or simply blowing your nose. You try to bring sad thoughts to mind hoping to divert your attention, but nothing seems to suffocate that tormenting guffaw that seems to be screaming, "Let me out, or I'll huff and I'll puff and I'll blow you right out of this uncomfortable, wooden pew!"

Sitting in my usual center aisle, fifth row pew, one Sunday morning, I was pleased to see that both the choir and the bell ringers would be leading us in worship. That was always a special treat. Sixty-five men and women impressively dressed in royal blue choir robes with white collars stood motionless, eyes glued attentively to the very precise and impeccably dressed director who would give them the cue to break into a resounding chorus of "Praise to the Lord, the Almighty, the King of Creation! O my soul praise Him for He is our help and salvation!"

Directly in front of the choir were twelve bell ringers wearing full length black skirts, white blouses with red neck bows and spotless white gloves. They, too, stood in perfect attention waiting patiently for their own signal to join in the happy celebration of music. At the first nod from the leader, all the members picked up their shiny brass instruments by the handles and in perfect unison lifted them up to their shoulders in eager anticipation of providing beautiful tones to blend in with the symphony of voices coming from directly behind them.

Sue, a most accomplished senior bell ringer, apparently had just a little too much gusto that morning. As she picked up four of the smaller sized bells and lifted them up, two of them flew out of her hand and went sailing out of control, heading straight for the packed choir loft. Suddenly, right in the middle of "Praise to the Lord, who o'er all things so wondrously reigneth . . . " half a dozen blue robes ducked down to avoid the airborne weapons heading unsteadily in their direction. One of the taller singers, obviously a sports fan, reached out to grab bell number one like an avid spectator at a ball game reaching for a fly ball. Unfortunately, in the process, he knocked the songbook out of the hand of his tenor neighbor who reeled a bit, then unexpectedly hit a particularly high note and staggered to stay on his feet. The second bell landed first, on a metal music stand then on the floor with a loud echoing 'bong, boong, booong' that reverberated throughout the crowded sanctuary.

The startled but good-natured director continued to lead the choir with as much composure as he could possibly rally under the circumstances. Since the bell ringers couldn't play with the missing notes, he motioned to a choir member, a short little lady in the front row, to retrieve both bells. The woman disappeared from view as she groped on the floor to find the second bell. But after several seconds she emerged empty handed. Shrugging her shoulders, she returned to her place with the choir. Finally, one of the ringers spotted the shiny instrument near the pulpit. He broke rank, grabbed the elusive bell and with a grin from ear to ear, handed it back to a very flustered and embarrassed Sue who probably was wishing by then that she'd stayed in bed that morning.

The entire fiasco was a comedy of errors that stilled the voices of one or two choir members. The tall sports fan had to excuse himself, because regardless of how hard he tried to sing, every time he opened his mouth he broke into a fit of laughter. By then most of the congregation had lost control and broke into hysterics.

At that point the director stopped the music and after cracking up himself, he announced; "Okay now, take two! Everybody take a deep breath and let's try again."

Sue and her fellow bell ringers were able to get through the entire musical number but not without a good deal of noticeable, smothered giggling.

Somehow, I have a feeling that our Omniscient Lord knew our intentions were good. He knew that our worship was meant to be sincere and our laughter had nothing to do with irreverence or disrespect for His Holiness. Laughter in that kind of situation was healthy, natural and appropriate. Responding in any other way would have been abnormal.

Unquestionably, the Holiness of God is a call for awesome, reverent worship. Our God is the King of Kings that Isaiah refers to as he reveals a vision given to him by the Lord in Isaiah 6:1-5.

"In the year that King Uzziah died, I saw the Lord sitting on a throne, high and exalted, and the train of His robe filled the temple." (Isaiah 6:1)

The vision Isaiah sees is one of the glorious Majesty and the proper response to His Majesty is total respect, fear and reverence for the One who has all authority in heaven and on earth.

"Therefore, since we receive a kingdom which cannot be shaken, let us show gratitude, by which we may offer to God an acceptable service with reverence and awe." (Hebrews 12:28)

The people of God can sometimes gather together for sincere worship before a Holy God when out of the blue something ridiculously unexpected happens and sends everyone into convulsive laughter. The congregation, including the leaders, then runs the risk of being criticized and judged as frivolous and even irreverent in its worship, by sober, long-faced members of the flock, who look at humor in church as the 'unpardonable sin.' Where does that leave the joy of the Lord? Joy often brings with it laughter, and laughter is often spontaneous. Laughter also has been proven to be beneficial therapy.

A sense of humor is a precious gift given to us by God to release tensions and put things in perspective. The tediousness of ho-hum everyday living in a fallen world becomes less difficult and burdensome if it's tempered with laughter.

"A happy heart makes the face cheerful, but heartache crushes the spirit." (Proverbs 15:13)

"Every good gift and every perfect gift is from above, and comes down from the Father of lights, with whom there is no variation or shadow of turning." (James 1:17)

I expect that *'Yahweh'* in all of His glory was laughing right along with all of us the day the bells went flying.

Several ministers I've known and others I've only read about, like to interject humor into their sermons. Charles Spurgeon was no slouch in that area. He was a man of good cheer and he frequently had the congregation in stitches by giving them an account of something that struck him especially funny during the course of the week, always using the story as an illustration to make a point.

Warren Wiersbe tells a funny story about a man who was under the false impression that he was the most interesting conversationalist the world had ever known, simply because he'd been privileged to have done some extensive traveling. Mr. Wiersbe goes on to say, "If you put a jackass on a plane in Texas and send him around the world, he will still be a jackass when he returns. He simply will have put distance under his feet and even a common duck can do the same."

Personally, the sound of laughter coming from a congregation is much more appealing to me than the sound of a bored parishioner's untimely snoring. Preceding a sermon with a funny anecdote will often be helpful in emphasizing the main point.

Recently I was listening to a taped sermon from a pastor speaking on the willingness to accept changes in our lives and being able to adjust to accommodate those changes. "God has little use for people who are unwilling or unable to accept change," he warned.

To the delight of his church family, he spoke of moving from a metropolitan area near Washington, D.C., to a rural area in Southeast Iowa, where cornfields line the tranquil countryside and a high rise is only a term to describe the size of the crops. Lying in bed the first night in their new home, windows were open to allow the crispness of the Fall air to come in. This pastor was meditating on the joy of living in a place where, the livin' is easy and the corn is high. Listening to the pleasant sounds of noisy crickets, nocturnal animals and the rustling of Autumn leaves, he thanked God for having brought him to this lovely place and for the quietness of his new neighborhood. Within minutes he was lulled into a peaceful sleep. Before he had a chance to start dreaming, he was unmercifully jolted out of a dead sleep by a penetrating whistle and the 'chug, chug, chugging' of an endless train that seemed to be taking a shortcut right through the master bedroom. He jumped out of bed and screamed to his wife and children, "Quick, get up, everybody outdoors! We've bought a house on a railroad track!!!"

The pews, filled with several hundred Iowans, roared at his story. They were well accustomed to the loud whistle of a train and never thought anything about them.

The pastor went on to explain that after two weeks, the trains were still coming several times a night, but he never heard them anymore. Rather than lying awake listening for the whistles and getting angry, he'd gotten used to them and even began to enjoy the chug-chug-chugging sound. His story was funny and brief and was only an introduction to a deeper spiritual insight.

Humor makes a pastor real and relatable before the people. It can be the spice that makes a sermon come alive and keeps people sitting on the edge of their seats wanting to hear more. It should never be the focus of a message but only a tool to build upon.

Yes, laughter, in moderation, is appropriate even in the pulpit.

There is, however, a fine line and a delicate balance that must be observed by pastors, speakers, teachers and even Christian comedians. All have a responsibility before God to find that balance and adhere to it. We are, after all, accountable to our Most Holy God to rightly divide the Word and to spread it.

Some Christian speakers have been known to be so funny that the Word of God can become totally obscured. The message becomes absorbed or overshadowed by the jokes. The audience then leaves having had a barrel of laughs but having been fed nothing. Stomachs may have been filled with a potpourri of exotic foods, but the spiritual buffet table was empty as if the host had not even a crumb to offer. How is that different from the comedy clubs of the world?

A few years ago I attended a Christian luncheon with five hundred women in attendance, a number of them were either new believers or unbelievers. It was to be an evangelistic outreach. The speaker was well known for her comical deliveries. What an opportunity, I thought, to reach a large group of women with the Gospel message in a non-threatening way. For almost an hour the speaker had everyone in stitches. She never stopped. Her expressions and her stories were truly side-splitting. She was a one-woman show and clearly gifted. But if there was a Godly message given in that hour, I missed it, and the Gospel was never presented. Listening to the comments of women on the way out, my heart sank at the thought of a missed opportunity. All I heard was, "That's one funny lady!"—"She's a riot!"—"Wasn't that fun?"

Like all other gifts, the gift of humor comes directly from God. We can thank Him and give back to Him by refining that gift to the best of our ability and use it to bring honor and glory to His Name. To do otherwise is to bring glory to ourselves, that precious gift then becomes only temporal and has no eternal value. Sometimes laughter, when it's overdone, is simply not appropriate.

The Christian life does give us the freedom to enjoy life to the fullest. That was Christ's dying wish for us as He prayed to the Father just before the crucifixion.

"I am coming to you now, but I say these things while I am still in the world, so that they may have the full measure of my joy within them." (John 17:13)

Having the full measure of His joy includes laughter and the wisdom to discern when it's appropriate and when it's not.

On a lighter note, the following is a list of times when laughter would be considered appropriate and when it might not be. I know all of these things can happen because all of them have actually happened to me at one time or another.

— TO LAUGH —

You get up in the morning and think you're going blind, then, just when you're about to call the doctor, you find that a lens has fallen out of your eyeglasses.

You try to straighten out the wrinkles in your panty hose and you realize you're not wearing any.

You come home from the local consignment shop excited about the small price you paid for a blouse—then you find out it's the same blouse you gave them the previous week because it didn't fit right.

You go to the drive-through at the bank and try to put the tube back in the cylinder. Because you are so short, you have to unhook your seatbelt and stretch as far as you can and fall out of your car.

You have to leave your prayer group alone in your home because you have a doctor's appointment. This saintly group decides to pull a practical joke on you. They get into your underwear drawer and cover the living room of your home with underpants, bras, and the like. When you arrive home the UPS man is in your driveway so you invite him in to drop off the package. When you walk in with this stranger, there are unmentionables hanging from chandeliers, banisters, ceiling fans and everywhere you can imagine. There's no way to explain this interesting display so you just smile, sign the papers, say goodbye, and send the puzzled UPS man on his way.

— NOT TO LAUGH —

You wake up from major surgery and you can hear someone playing the harp in your room.

You ask a total stranger, "Have you seen my car?" because you know you parked it somewhere at "Mall USA", but where?

You're walking out of church wearing a knee length dress and your half slip suddenly drops down to your ankles.

You invite your friend to a wedding and after the minister gives the blessing for the food, she breaks into loud applause. He prayed so long, she thought it was a short sermon.

You put four potatoes in the oven for guests but when they're done you're one short. You find the fourth one when you cut into the chocolate cake you baked for dessert.

You thank the church organist for her rendition of the Lord's Prayer, she says thank you but that's not what she played.

CHAPTER FIVE

One Size Fits All

✼ *Veda Boyd* ✼

"Smiles come preshrunk; you can wash them with hot water and they will still fit your face."
- Veda Boyd

Smiles, unlike certain articles of clothing, can be worn by just about anyone, at anytime, and virtually in every place. Any size smile looks good on any size face . . . not at all like other things I've tried on . . . and off . . . and on . . . and off.

Have you ever watched . . . I mean really watched . . . someone smile? Have you discovered that pair of eyes that instantly light up at the slightest tug on their funny bone?

Working in an orthodontic office, where I not only come in contact with hundreds of children and adults, but also with the same number of facial expressions, I have had hundreds of opportunities to observe people's faces—especially those of young children.

More recently, it was the face of my new month-old granddaughter, Fiona, that I watched. Observing this precious gift of joy who had entered the world prematurely, I saw the face of an angel. I saw the same thing on the faces of my first two grandchildren and it brought a super-sized smile to my face.

Whether Fiona was sound asleep, or as awake as any month-old baby can be, the curl of her mouth, the quiver of her lips and the innocence of her eyes, captured my heart. What is seen in our faces can enthrall onlookers, or it can have the opposite affect, but in the case of Fiona, she enthralled me even before she could walk or talk. The face is the canvas on which our thoughts and the contents of our hearts are portrayed. Monet, eat your heart out!

There is one particular young girl, named Laura, in our orthodontic office who comes to my mind when I think of what a face can portray. When Laura smiles (in spite of a mouth full of metal braces), her eyes literally disappear, and in their place, sunbeams appear. I have never seen a sweeter dimple-faced young girl whose eyes sparkle more than 4th of July sparklers. Every time you speak to her, or her two brothers, Luke and John, they don jovial smiles and equally pleasant dispositions. Such joyful expressions make me want to be around them, to talk with them, and to listen to them. The origin of their joy, as I discovered, is a close relationship with Jesus and devoted parental love and godly discipline. Such joy is contagious.

I'm convinced that, according to the Word of God, *"The cheerful heart has a continual feast." (Proverbs 15:15)* A life satisfied with feasting on God's goodness results in a joyful disposition. Conversely, others wear emaciated complexions due to the spiritual dehydration in their lives; they are void of joy! Valium, or other La-La producing drugs, seem to be much more appealing than a hefty dose of laughter for some people. Why is that? Are they merely shopping for the right size smile, and still haven't found it?

A smile from the heart is like a magnet that draws you to it; you are eager to find out what lies beyond and beneath the smile. Whether it is gentle and warm or beaming and brilliant, a smile is captivating, and so are the people who wear them. Helen Keller is quoted as saying: "Keep your face to the sunshine and you cannot see the shadow." Despite her blindness, she knew the significance of a warm smile and a caring heart.

"Cheerfulness is no sin, nor is there any grace in a solemn cast of countenance." Jon Newton (1725-1807)

In the book of Luke, when the prodigal son returns home, his father doesn't wait until he comes up the front steps of the porch to greet him. Instead, he runs to meet him—a good distance down the road. I can well imagine the happiness and exuberant laughter mingled with overflowing tears of joy as he got closer and closer to his returning son. *". . . For this son of mine was dead and has come to life again; he was lost and has been found. And they began to celebrate."* (Luke 15:24)

I realize Scripture doesn't say that the young man's father laughed, but if you are a mother or father of a prodigal son or daughter, I feel safe in saying that, you would laugh, shout, cry and probably beat your chest like a drum, if you saw your child coming home, after a season of sin! So I don't think it would be off the wall to suggest that there was some laughter heard at that reunion!

A reunion between a wayward husband or wife whose sin of folly is finally acknowledged and repented of, would warrant that same kind of celebration, don't you think?

There is joy in obedience! Healing is not just for the scrapes and scratches of everyday living, with its disappointments and sorrows, but it is also for the deep wounds, the unspeakable injuries, and the unexpected betrayals. The scabs will fall off, the scars will grow lighter—if they don't disappear altogether—but a smile will return when all is well with your soul. At first, the smile may be small, nearly unrecognizable, but it will widen as your heart changes from unforgiveness to forgiveness and from disobedience to obedience.

Smiles do not take a whole lot of energy. That being so, you'd think smiles would be more common, wouldn't you? Some people, however, appear to require NASA rocket-boosters to launch a smile on their faces. I have had many encounters with unsmiling human beings. I say encounters, because I really had no desire to have close-encounters with them. Some of those people, I sadly report, were Christians. I have also met many more that wouldn't be caught dead laughing out-loud. Well, they needn't worry, I suppose, because morticians have a way of removing every smile from your face anyway! How often have you witnessed a deceased body with a smile on its face, even if you were confident they had already entered the gates of heaven? OK, maybe there was a highly paid, half-hearted attempt at producing one, but instead, they always end up looking like they are squeezing back some important last words to the mortician, like: "I'm a Christian, make me smile!"

Laughs, styles of laughter, and smiles, are as varied as sneezes. When my mother used to sneeze, I was certain she was no larger than a grasshopper. It squeaked out, had no punch and never left anyone feeling like they had been given a shower. It was cute, though. Her laugh wasn't much different than her sneeze. If she had worn a laugh barometer, the needle would never have moved. I'm sure you know people like that. They take every precaution to suppress their sneezes and their joy, for fear someone might consider them unspiritual and/or unruly. I feel sorry for people like that, because I think they are missing out on something really healthy. Lest I be misunderstood, I loved my foster mother, no matter what size smile she wore or the amount of "spritz" that emanated from her sneeze.

On occasion, my mother would break out in a hearty laugh, but we always made sure it wasn't on the day the Bishop was planning a visit. She kept her laughs and smiles lady-like most of the time, but she confessed to me that she always felt so much better when she could laugh and sneeze really loud! I loved her for that. Her smile was a size small, but it touched many people with its warmth and sincerity. It is not the size of the smile that is important, as long as you smile.

In Philippians 1:25-26, Paul was talking about the gospel and wanting to go be with the Lord, but finding it more beneficial to the body of believers to remain behind. He said, "*. . . I know that I shall remain and continue with you for your progress and JOY in the faith.*" Did you get that? There is to be JOY in faith . . . not ragged-edged joy, but joy unspeakable! Are we not hearing Paul's words today?

When I laugh, I am quite often mistaken for Phyllis Diller. My laughter reverberates through buildings and echoes between mountaintops. My laugh happens to come from the floor of my bowels . . . most of the time. And I must mention that most of my children have inherited my laughing genes. When I reckon something to be funny, everyone knows it. It's not that I try and be the loudest person in the room, I just am. I have never learned to hold anything back (I've proven that by the number of Hershey Kisses I have eaten in one sitting). My laugh is XXXL.

When my best friend, co-author of this book and I get together to practice for presentations, I always end up laughing so hard that I actually hurt all over. It's not that I enjoy hurting, but laughing happens to affect every part of my body that way. When we pray, or when we eat, we do it all to the glory of God and we do it with equal enthusiasm!

On one occasion, while practicing for a skit we had been asked to do, I was supposed to make an entrance carrying a tray containing two cups of tea. My first line, as I entered the room was supposed to be, "Hi Odds!" to while she was to reply, "Hi Ends!" But when my friend looked up at me in her long black wig and baseball cap, making her look more like a witch than my very best friend (which was in itself enough to have me on the floor laughing), she replied, "Hi Evens!" She had forgotten the name of our duo team: "Odds and Ends" and renamed us "Odds and Evens." It was all over after that; practicing was just not going to be productive that day. My stomach jogged at least five miles over that faux pas.

I think of Sarah in Genesis 21:6 "**after**" giving birth to her son Isaac, when she said, *"God has made laughter for me; everyone who hears will laugh with me."* She herself had laughed **before** her son was born, because of her and her husband's "way-beyond child-bearing years." Now she was laughing because God had fulfilled His promise to them, and there they were with a new baby boy! I'll tell you what, after waiting for, and sometimes probably doubting God's promise to give them a child, the size of her laugh must have doubled. It is enough to express joy over a promise fulfilled, but to have a new baby, at that age, added to Sarah's heartfelt laughter.

The joy of the Lord is irresistible! That's why Sarah must have known that others would laugh with her. You might be saying about now, "Well, you don't have to be a Christian to laugh; I know lots of people who aren't Christians, and they laugh." You're right, they do . . . but as far as God is concerned, their life here on earth will be the last time they laugh or experience joy, if they are living without Him. Christians (people who have a personal relationship with Jesus Christ), will enjoy "joy" for an eternity! Our joy will only increase. But thank God, it's never too late (unless you are dead), to receive the gift of eternal life, which translates into eternal joy.

Then there are those who laugh, and you know they don't mean it . . . a sort of polite ha-ha. Yes, you know a few of those, don't you? You wonder why they even bother. In that case, a shallow response is not better than no-response at all; you know that person should be laughing . . . they are looking at you! Sometimes, don't you just want to take your fingers and stretch their mouth into the shape of a wide smile, showing all of their teeth, because it's apparent that they can't do it for themselves? I also think those non-smilers should hang signs on their doors: IGNORE THE DOG BUT BEWARE OF THE JOY KILLER INSIDE!

There are things that can make you grin, smile and laugh . . . and reasons for all three are as different as the size of your reaction . . . from person to person and circumstance to circumstance. What is most important is that, something in your life is worth making you smile or laugh. If there isn't, your life may need spiritual fine-tuning. Then again, maybe you are one of those people who get joy only out of what the world has to offer, or when other people make fools of themselves, and you know nothing of the joy of Jesus. In that case, I recommend you seek out a quiet place where you can ask Jesus into your life and to ask for forgiveness for your sins. Ask Him to fill your life with the joy of His salvation . . . the joy of the Lord; lasting joy!

"Let your light shine before men in such a way that they may see your good works, and glorify your Father who is in heaven." (Matthew 5:16) As Christians, the world needs to see the SON shining in our lives!

Let me ask you something: Would you prefer being around someone who is joyful over someone whose mouth resembles a door arch? I would. But I have also discovered that it is much easier to share someone's sadness than it is to share their joy. Have you ever known someone who has accomplished something really significant, a moment of sheer happiness and joy for that person? Have you noticed that very few people rejoice along with them over their accomplishment? The envy factor arrives on the scene almost immediately—like a villain that missed his cue in a three-act play, ruining a perfectly good act. The star, in this case—the person who has accomplished something notable—is left with just a few close friends with whom they can rejoice. On the other hand, it's a lot easier to sympathize with someone, who has experienced a loss, or failed at that long hoped-for achievement or for the villain who bungled his lines; there is no competition, no threat, and no feeling of envy anywhere in the midst of loss. That is where you will discover crowds of sympathizers, contrary to the size of the crowd sharing in your joy. The size of our love can easily be measured by how we share in another's joy, as well as in their grief. Sharing a laugh, or a tear, requires putting yourself in that person's situation, or loving them so much that you can feel their joy and their pain.

I believe that, as children of God, we can appreciate that truth. Jesus suffered terribly for us, and we feel that pain when we recognize our own sin—the reason He had to die on the cross in the first place. Then we rejoice when we learn and believe, according to Scripture, that He arose from the grave and took His place at the right hand of God, the Father, in Heaven, where He is now interceding for you and me. Alleluia! He made a way, where there was no other way. Our response should be XXXL in gratitude and joy.

I love to make people laugh. From the time I was a young girl, I loved to see people happy, especially if I contributed to the reason for their laughter. It is not much different today. In the ministry of "Odds and Ends," the opportunities for all sizes of laughter have increased, and I find that in making others laugh, I get happy, too.

Recently, while on a speaking weekend in Ocean City, Maryland, I roomed with my ministry partner "Ret." We are two peas in a pod, yet different in so many ways. We wake up at the same time in the middle of the night, in pain of one sort or another. We end up laughing at our discomfort, and it does make the pain seem less painful. I suspect the proverbial saying "Misery loves company" isn't far from the truth. Our discomfort has given us many humorous stories to share with women, and most understand what we're talking about. On that particular speaking engagement, "Ret" revealed to a conference room full of ladies that I had a bad back. My response was, "I may have a bad back, but I have a terrific front!" It brought the house down. You know, we are so uptight sometimes that we miss the fun in our own discomfort.

I truly believe Jesus is in the midst of both joy and pain. He says that *"where two or more are gathered together, there I am, in the midst of them." (Matthew 18:20)* I do not believe He would excuse Himself if those gatherers broke out in king-size laughter, anymore than He would take leave if they were praying and crying together.

"These things I have spoken to you, that in Me you may have peace. In the world you have tribulation, but take courage; I have overcome the world." (John 16:33) Could there be any better reason for victorious living and laughing? He has overcome the world; we are on the winning grinning side!

". . . For the Lord God is my strength and song, and He has become my salvation. Therefore, you will joyously draw water from the springs of salvation. (Isaiah 12:2-3)

". . . My mouth offers praises with joyful lips." (Psalm 63:5b)

"For You have been my help, and in the shadow of Your wings I sing for joy." (Psalm 63:7)

Should we walk around with perpetual smiles on our faces? No, that is not what I am implying, nor is it implied in the quoted Scripture verses, but neither should we be perpetually sad. *"For His anger is but for a moment; His favor is for a lifetime; Weeping may last for the night, but a shout of joy comes in the morning." (Psalm 30:5)*

You will not find an excuse in this chapter for a continual down-in-the-mouth attitude (unless you're a dentist, oral surgeon or ENT), so you may want to consider smiling. It's Biblical and one size fits all!

At one point in my life, someone handed me a piece of paper with this quote from Chuck Swindoll: "We have no more right to put our discordant states of mind into the lives of those around us and rob them of their sunshine and brightness than we have to enter their houses and steal their silverware!" Some people are eating with plastic knives and forks because they no longer have silverware. They have been robbed of joy and they aren't even trying to get it back.

After reading that quote, I thought, *how true; I need a faith-lift and reconstruction of my attitude.* That advice has been instrumental in changing my attitude to this very day.

There are still times when circumstances make me very sad, to the point of being downright pained, but most of the time, I do not lament over things that I cannot change, especially the things that pertain to me. But, I do hurt deeply for others. It is worse when there is nothing I can do about their situations, and I must finally take it and lay it at the cross and tell Jesus that I must completely trust Him. That is when He begins to heal my hurting heart, as I give the lives of those for whom I hurt, into His loving hands. What we can do, however, is pray. It's a command from above, and it's what God wants us to do. For the war on sorrow and despair, we go armed with prayer! Amen?

There is a friend of mine, with whom I have often shared, a lack of sympathy and compassion for complaining and disorganized people, people who are hard pressed to laugh in any size, at any time. We admitted to one another that we do not have the gift of compassion. Not that we don't care about those people, but we just can't understand why anyone would want to roll around in the muck and mire of their circumstances without the willingness to change, either their circumstances, or their attitudes. We try and practice compassion and understanding, hoping to be more like Jesus, but we fail quite often, but we don't give up. Left on our own, we would avoid contact with those people, but we are challenged on such occasions to show compassion, as two women who have been shown compassion by Jesus.

"You oh Lord, will not withhold Your compassion from me; Your loving kindness and Your truth will continually preserve me." (Psalm 40:11)

Looking into the faces of people often time pains me, and pains me greatly. While they are talking joy, they show something else. Why is it so hard for people to put on a smile? It's a little like setting a beautiful table, with fresh flowers and lovely dinnerware, and then serving mud-pies. I often find myself not believing what those people say. Someone, to whom I spoke regarding their countenance once said, "Oh, I was born with this look." H-E-L-L-O! I was born thin too, but I did something about it. If we remained as we were, when we were born, we'd all still be shaking rattles and eating Pabulum. Not me, I want to feast on steak, hard-shell crabs, and the fullness of His joy! Spiritual thinness is not attractive and cannot be a satisfying way to exist. God wants so much more for His children. Go shopping! Smiles are free!

In the Scriptures, we are encouraged to make a joyful noise unto the Lord, yet, the world is fraught with critics of spiritual expression who have settled for only secular joyful noise. I don't think laughter, hand raising, hand clapping, or even contemporary music, done in an orderly fashion, will get on God's nerves. I am sure that the size of our laughter and the expressions of our hearts will indicate the breadth and depth of the joy that we have "in" Him.

When you hear a hearty laugh . . . from the bowels, or from any other bodily location, don't be too critical. Allow yourself the God-given liberty to laugh, no matter what size it is; you won't even have to try it on . . . it is guaranteed to fit!

CHAPTER SIX

Suppose I'm Not Funny

🦋 *Laurette Connelly* 🦋

My friends and I were fortunate to have spent a week at a popular Christian conference center this past summer. At every meal we sat with a different group of people getting to know each other and sharing a bit about ourselves. One woman, whom I will refer to only as Clara, joined us on two separate occasions. We also ran into her several times during the course of our stay. At first we got to know very little about Clara except that she loved to tell jokes. Unfortunately, she very often forgot the punchline or would get it so mixed up that it only was funny to her. Clara had a wonderful sense of humor but she sadly lacked the *gift* of humor. She really cracked herself up but left a trail of perplexed people in her wake.

I would love to have Clara in the audience when I tell a funny story because she would be responsive and easily amused. But she would unquestionably fare better in the audience rather than on the stage. Clara did endear herself to us because she seemed to be having such a great time. Nevertheless, she needs to use the gift that God has given to her and focus on polishing that gift rather than abrasively subjecting others to an area where she is clearly not gifted.

Later in the week, after asking a number of questions, we found that Clara had been blessed with the voice of an angel. She was a very creative gardener and decorator as well as being an avid golfer. Clara was an intelligent and sharp woman who had in no way been short-changed in the gift department.

As children of God, we've all been given different gifts. Not one of us is lacking. One gift is not more important than the other. Whether a gift is an up-front gift or behind the scenes is incidental. All the gifts work together to accomplish God's purposes in this world. One can hardly function without the other. A speaker has no platform without someone operating the sound system. A vocalist can't sing without music. Churches can't operate without nursery workers or dedicated kitchen help. Without each other we are as useless as a bell choir with missing bells.

"But to each one of us grace has been given as Christ apportioned it. This is why it says: 'When he ascended on high, he led captives in his train and gave gifts to men.'" (Ephesians 4:7-8)

My friend Rose is a compassionate, godly woman. God has blessed her with the gifts of teaching, mercy, wisdom and many others. She has not, however, been given the gift of humor. Rose inspires me and challenges me in areas I would never have approached. She stretches me, but she does not make me laugh, that's not what Rose brings into our friendship. But Rose and I can still have fun together because she has a sense of humor and she can laugh until the tears roll down her cheeks at some of the stupid things I often manage to get myself into.

Having a sense of humor does not require that one possess the gift of humor. We have not all received that gift any more than we can all sing or play an instrument. God has not gifted me with musical abilities, as all who know me will be quick to attest. When I sang lullabies to my babies they cried and went to sleep when I stopped. When they were old enough to speak they boldly said, "Mommy, don't sing, please don't sing, I'll go to sleep." I love nothing better than listening to gifted singers. While I recognize that God did not gift me in that area, I can truly appreciate the talent with which someone else has been blessed.

Playing an instrument is a secret ambition of mine and I'm hoping that in heaven I'll play the flute like my friend Gail does. Every year at Christmas I would ask my husband to buy me an organ with numbers written on the keys. "I'll teach myself to play," I pleaded.

Eventually John gave in and bought me a small Hammond organ and several "play by number" music books. Wisely, he also bought me earphones so the family would not have to suffer through my feeble attempts at playing *"Silent Night"* or *"Walking in the Winter Wonderland,"* until the warmth of Spring, when thoughts turn to popping daffodils, tulips and blossoms on weeping cherry trees. I wondered if DaVinci painted *"The Last Supper"* by number . . . Hmmm.

With the purchase of my prized organ I was entitled to receive twelve free lessons at the local mall. Determined to become a brilliant organist, I attended every lesson and practiced diligently in between. On the final night of lessons, all the students were asked to play the piece they had practiced. It was our first informal recital and we were all chomping at the bit to show off the progress we had made since our initial meeting.

The first young man, a tall gangly kid with long hair, a hoop in his nose and braces on his teeth, took his seat at the instrument not unlike "Liberace" doing a concert at Carnegie Hall. The only thing missing was the ornate candelabra and the sequined costume. Placing his long fingers confidently on the keyboard he hesitated dramatically then played a flawless rendition of *"Amazing Grace"* with a Spanish beat. When he finished, the crowd of shoppers who gathered to hear him play, encouraged by the proud teacher, broke into grateful applause. I heard one woman shout "Bravo!" Another yelled "Encore!" Wow! I could hardly wait for my turn, I knew I would knock their socks off.

The second woman I don't even want to talk about, I know she cheated. She had to have at least fifteen lessons. *Probably private ones*, I thought, she seemed to me to be a little too cozy with the teacher. The crowd not only lingered and applauded while she was still playing *"Let Me Call You Sweetheart"* but couples began to find partners to dance with while humming the tune as they twirled their partners on the makeshift dance floor.

Finally, it was my turn. I had been practicing *"Silent Night"* for weeks. *"Easter Bonnet"* would have been more appropriate, but I wasn't there yet. I sat and smiled nervously at the crowd of onlookers and that was the last I saw of them. When I looked up, they had all vanished. *Come back here, I'm not finished!* I wanted to yell. One of the other students was singing along with me but he was way off key and he couldn't keep up with me. The teacher looked like he was going to be sick. "Mrs. Connelly," he said, "maybe you ought to consider taking the extended course. I'm not sure but it's possible that another thirty lessons could be helpful."

That was the end of my musical career. I still love to listen to a good organist. I have a sincere appreciation for their abilities, but I've come to the stark realization that I will never be counted as one of them, regardless of how many lessons I take. I have trouble in church when we're asked to clap to the beat while singing praise songs. I can't do both—sing and clap—that's asking too much of me!!!

My point is that we can fully enjoy *all* the gifts that God has given to any of His children. Some we enjoy as active participants and others as grateful recipients.

The gift of humor probably can't be acquired anymore than I could become a good organist, but a sense of humor can definitely be developed. The first thing we need to do is look for humor in everyday living. Laugh at life, laugh at yourself and laugh with others. Laughing is more than fun. It's healthy, it's good exercise and it's all around us, it's in the supermarket, in your home, in your church, in the classroom, it's everywhere.

Someone once said that if you learn to laugh at yourself, you would always be amused.

After celebrating Mother's Day with my daughter, Sheila and her family in Downingtown, Pa, I was heading home about 2:30 p.m. on a beautiful, sunny afternoon and decided to take the scenic route rather than a busy highway. As I was approaching a nearby town, a giant truck obscured by view. All I could see for several miles was the rear end of the annoying eighteen-wheeler in front of me with its bold, large letters that asked, "HOW'S MY DRIVING? CALL 1-800 FOR DRIVE."

As we approached a nearby town several uniformed policemen lined the streets where traffic was at a standstill. Clearly something was going on, whatever it was, was a mystery to me. To my surprise, one of the policemen blew his whistle and motioned for the truck in front of me to make a left turn at the next corner. Assuming that all traffic was being re-routed, I, of course, followed right along. *Must be a major accident,* I thought, sending up a quick prayer for the unfortunate victims.

After driving for another block, I realized this was not an accident at all, but a very big festive parade and I somehow found myself right in the middle of it. I was part of the parade with no way of escape because all the streets were blocked off.

Spectators lined the streets three and four deep. Young and old alike waved flags and threw confetti in every direction. Children held onto colorful, helium-filled balloons while the smell of cotton candy and freshly popped corn permeated the air.

Beautifully decorated trucks and floats traveled before me, joyfully honking noisy horns to the delight of the little tykes along the route. A precision high school marching band in blue and gold uniforms paraded proudly behind me, led by a most enthusiastic drum majorette wearing a tall fur hat that seemed to swallow her face and hold her chin in place. Directly behind her were three accomplished baton twirlers, their chests covered with shiny medals. The girls could send those silver sticks flying almost into the clouds, do a couple of spins or handstands wait a few minutes and have them land precisely into their nimble fingers. It was like magic!

Sandwiched between the trucks and the spinning magicians I decided there was only one thing to do. I had to act like I belonged. The large brimmed hat I'd worn to church that morning sat on the seat beside me, it would give credibility to my presence. Plopping the hat on my head just a tad askew, I opened the sunroof on my car and rolled down all the windows, I leaned on my horn and began to wave at the smiling jovial crowd like an ambitious politician out to get precious votes. Occasionally, I blew a kiss at a small child. Men, women, and children graciously waved back. Some blew kisses probably convinced that I was someone with a certain degree of importance, but who? Did anyone know?

For the next three miles I could hardly contain myself, sometimes laughing out loud at the ridiculousness of this situation. If these people only knew that I was nothing but a misdirected, lost old lady who didn't even know what town I was in or what this parade was all about. But I looked good, and may have enjoyed the parade more than anyone on the sidelines.

Laughing at yourself is good medicine. Solomon tells us that without it you can develop osteoporosis.

"A cheerful heart is good medicine, but a crushed spirit dries up the bones." (Proverbs 17:22)

The blows of life become a lot less painful when we learn to filter them with humor. The joy of life with Jesus is the pathway to release us from the bondage of a sober, somber and fearful existence. Jesus does not expect or want us to carry the cares of the world on our shoulders. To allow ourselves to be laden down with burdens is to not trust that He is able to do as He promised, and it is to hinder the work of the Holy Spirit in our everyday lives.

"Come to me, all you who are weary and burdened, and I will give you rest. Take my yoke upon you and learn from me, for I am gentle and humble in heart, and you will find rest for your souls. For my yoke is easy and my burden is light." (Matthew 11:28, 30)

"Which of you by worrying can add a single hour to his life?" (Matthew 6:27)

"Therefore do not worry about tomorrow, for tomorrow will worry about itself. Each day has enough trouble of its own." (Matthew 6:34)

There's much truth to the old song *"It isn't any trouble just to S-M-I-L-E, so smile when you're in trouble, it will vanish like a bubble if you only take the trouble just to S-M-I-L-E!"* . . . A smile never goes out of style. It's been recognized as a sign of friendship by every generation since time began. A smile has the power to make another person's face light up. It's a way of reflecting the joy of the Lord and maybe even in a small way help lighten someone's burden. Best of all, it doesn't cost a thing and brings lasting and valuable rewards.

A few months ago I received a sweet thank you note from a lady at my church thanking me for saying "good morning" and smiling at her as I walked by. "That smile meant so much to me," she said. "I'm fairly new at the church and I was feeling lost and almost invisible amidst hundreds of people having friendly conversations. Your greeting made me feel less lonely and brought a feeling of joy to my heart."

What a humbling experience to know that such a simple gesture can make a difference in someone's life. The joy of the Lord is so easy to pass on, why do we so often hold back?

"Though you have not seen Him, you love Him; and even though you do not see Him now, you believe in Him and are filled with an inexpressible and glorious joy." (I Peter 1:8)

Inexpressible joy in Christ brings inexpressible freedom to allow that joy to spill over to others and even into our very soul and help us to see that life with Him becomes a laughing matter. Admittedly, it's far easier to thank Him for the laughter than it is for the agonizing tears that are sure to come. But He is Sovereign over it all, victories as well as trials.

Joy is not just a syrupy word to give us a warm fuzzy feeling. It's a way of life, it's the icing on our spiritual cake. We can have a joy-filled life in Christ even when the bottom falls out and it looks like we're going to make a crash landing in the sea of life.

I'm reminded of an unwed, pregnant teenage girl named Mary who was in a situation that would call for her to be stoned, according to the law. It couldn't have been all bells and whistles as she tried to explain to the man she was about to marry that though she was pregnant, she was still a virgin. Yes, she was pregnant and no, this was not his child. She'd never been with a man . . . *Hmmmmmm.* How could she make Joseph understand? She, after all, had seen and heard the angel sent by God and still it was hard for her, but Joseph had seen and heard nothing.

Mary accepted the challenge that would change her life forever. Upon hearing the announcement that she was to bear a child, she says simply, "I am the Lord's servant, and I will do whatever He desires."

Mary would be the Lord's servant even if it meant losing Joseph, even if it meant losing her reputation or her family. She expresses her joy powerfully in her beautiful *'Magnificat.'*

"My soul glorifies the Lord and my spirit rejoices in God my Savior, for He has been mindful of the humble state of His servant. From now on all generations will call me blessed, for the Mighty One has done great things for me—holy is His name." (Luke 1:46-49)

Mary didn't let her circumstances overtake her and throw her into a pit of hopeless depression. She knew the presence inside of her, was none other than her Savior, the promise of the ages, the Messiah of the world. She was filled with joy because she kept her mind on the hope that was hers in Him.

We, as believers in Christ have the same presence inside of us. Jesus tells us in John 14:18, *"I will not leave you orphans; I will come to you."*

". . . that they may all be one; even as you, Father, are in Me and I in you, that they also may be in Us, so that the world may believe that You sent Me." (John 17:21)

We have the same hope as Mary did. Should we not have the same joy? Can we say like Mary, *"My soul glorifies the Lord and my spirit rejoices in God my Savior?"*

CHAPTER SEVEN

Now Ain't That Funny

❋ *Veda Boyd* ❋

> "Laughter is the sun that drives
> winter from the human face."
> - Unknown Author

Someone once asked me this question: "What's so bad about being single?"

"Nothing," I replied, "that a little marriage wouldn't cure."

His response: "Now ain't that funny," made me laugh.

I admit; it doesn't take much to make me laugh, and my face is covered in laugh-lines to prove it! I know of no other creature on earth that has the ability to smile and laugh like humans do. Does that make you feel special? If it doesn't, it should.

Another information-generous person advised me to greet each morning by lying on my back and hanging my head over the side of the bed until my neck stretches beyond comfort. "Why in the world would I begin my day feeling like I'm in traction?" I questioned, quite stunned at the suggestion. Her point was; I could avoid developing a premature "turkey neck" (one full of furrows, sags and fat) by practicing this painful procedure every morning. Finding no other way to verbally express my aversion to her suggestion, I quickly replied, "I much prefer starting my day with a wide yawn, subdued lighting and a breath mint, thank you." Now ain't that funny!

Morning is actually very sacred to me, not for the reasons I've listed above, but because one of my favorite Bible verses guarantees me something to look forward to at the beginning of every day other than heart healthy instant oatmeal. *"The Lord's loving kindnesses indeed never cease, for His compassions never fail. They are new every morning; great is Your faithfulness." (Lamentations 3:22-23)* Instead of stretching my neck over the side of my bed, my faith gets stretched when I think upon these words and anticipate what God has for me each day.

How do you begin your day? Does your day begin trying to avoid an inevitable turkey-neck, or does it begin with high hopes and the promise of being covered in compassion and love by our Lord, all day long?

One thing I regularly anticipate every day, is an opportunity to laugh. There is a French proverb that says: "That day is lost on which one has not laughed." Being one-half French, I tend to agree with one-half of that Proverb. I don't think all is lost if you do not laugh every day, but if you do not laugh every day, it probably could have been a better day, had you laughed!

I used to sing in a church choir. At the end of one of our well-rehearsed and well- attended Christmas Cantatas, the choir members, and the pastor and his wife, were invited to enjoy refreshments at the home of a married choir-couple.

Not being entirely sure of the address where the get-together was going to be held, my friend and I engaged in numerous U-turns, reverse moves, and a dozen or more starts and stops until eventually we located the housing development where the home was purportedly located. With hands full of cake and other goodies, we approached the front door and let ourselves in, thinking everyone would be already busy preparing food and critiquing our musical performances.

My friend and I entered the home. In the darker-than-expected living room, we encountered a man and woman in their underwear, sitting on their respective recliner chairs, watching television. It didn't take gene research to know that our sense of direction had failed us. With red faces, we excused ourselves and tiptoed backwards out of the unfamiliar living room. Once outside, we could not contain our laughter. The tears rolled down our cheeks as we vividly recalled the look on the faces of those two unsuspecting television viewers. *What must they have thought?* we wondered! If it had been us, we decided, we would have screamed and dialed 911. But they had only sat there, noticeably unscathed by the intrusion. We were a bit concerned at the time that our unannounced appearance had sent them into a state of shock.

We realized then that the home where we were expected looked exactly like the home we had mistakenly entered. When we arrived at the correct home, we were relieved to find our group of choir members fully dressed and waiting for the rest of the guests to arrive.

As we began sharing our story (what could have been construed as "breaking and entering," by two upstanding church and choir members), and exactly what we had found upon entering the wrong residence, laughter began to fill the room.

Just then our pastor and his wife arrived.

It was only natural for them to inquire, before wiping their feet on the welcome mat, why the choir was engaged in hysterical laughter. When we relayed the story to them, they embarrassingly revealed to us that they too had gone to the wrong home and had encountered the same couple in their underwear watching TV.

That night, four people had invaded that couple's private home. Finding out that our pastor and his wife had done the same thing brought the house down. Albeit, the pastor and his wife were a lot more distressed over what had happened than my friend and I. Now ain't that funny!

Henry Ward Beecher once said: "Mirth is the sweet wine of human life. It should be offered sparkling with zestful life unto God." That night, a whole winery of mirth was offered unto God, and it is still being offered up every time we retell that embarrassing incident and begin to laugh all over again.

"But as for me, I shall sing of your strength; Yes, I shall joyfully sing of your loving kindness in the morning, For You have been my strong-

hold and a refuge in the day of my distress." (Psalm 59:16)

If you want to relieve yourself of stress (and four church members were indeed in need of stress relief after that encounter), sing a joyful song. Find something to laugh at, or someone to laugh with! Have you ever noticed how one song can lift you up and another bring you down? There is nothing that makes me feel worse than words to a song I can't understand (or wish I hadn't understood). But give me a good contemporary hymn, a classical rendition sung by Russell Watson, or a Ralph Carmichael Big Band Sound, and I'm on top of the world.

If you wonder why a great number of our youth are confused and in trouble, and the minds of our adults perverted, consider the words and visual conduct in the music they listen to and watch—the TV and Internet options available today. Where our minds and hearts dwell will pretty much be where our lives lead.

> "On this hapless earth
> There's small sincerity of mirth,
> And laughter oft is but an art
> To drown the outcry of our heart."
> - Hartley Coleridge

Have you ever been around someone with a nervous laugh? A laugh that you are sure is covering up pain? That would be the time to listen to that person, hear what they are trying to convey, and then come along side and journey with them on their road back to joy. "One's darkest hour," as the song goes, "is just before dawn."

One evening, I retired to my bedroom long before my typical midnight hour. I don't recall praying, but I do recall being exceptionally weary. It wasn't long before I entered the deep realm of sleep.

I began to stir as my rainforest-sounding-alarm-clock began to ring—about the time the morning sun usually warms the cement on my patio below. With greater alarm, I reached for my eyes, touching them, searching for an answer to why I could not see the face on my clock. All I could see was darkness. My eyes would not open. Seldom had I heard of people going blind overnight, but I was sure that I had. I knew that people died in their sleep, quite often in fact, and, for a moment, I thought I had died, but I was not seeing any of those bright lights you hear so much about nor had I encountered the face of God. Fearful that I had been unprepared to meet my Lord, I reached out and felt for my night table. *Yes,* I thought, *I am still in my bedroom. Now if only I can get to the bathroom. I'll be convinced I am not dead.* I can't explain why, but somehow the bathroom represented my presence in the physical "present." I couldn't recall standing before the Lord giving an account of my life; how much I loved, or what I did in the name of Jesus. *No, I was still alive;* I was fairly sure of that. But I had gone blind overnight and I was devastated.

When I reached the bathroom, by touch and feel, I located a washcloth. Saturating the cloth with very hot water, I held it to my eyes. Slowly, very slowly, my eyes began to open. At first, I saw only a thin blurred image of myself in the mirror ('thin' being definitely a mirage), then I began getting a bird's eye view of the countertop. I immediately noticed my contact lens case. The lids of each compartment were standing open and the little cups were definitely empty. Gratefully, I reached for the saline solution, filled the cups and began a rescue mission to retrieve my daily-wear-only contact lenses that I had neglected to remove before going to bed the night before. Delighted that I had only experienced temporary blindness; that my eyes had only been swollen shut from my extended wear of non-extended-wear contact lenses, I began to laugh. I was not laughing at my stupidity; I was laughing because I had not gone blind overnight, as I first suspected, and laughing was one way of expressing my relief and thankfulness proving there are many reasons to laugh. Now ain't that funny!

I thought of the story given to us in John 9 about the man who was blind from birth. People accused the blind man or his parents of sinning, reasoning why the man was born blind. But Jesus assured them: *"It was neither that this man sinned, nor his parents; but it was so that the works of God might be displayed in him. We must work the works of Him who sent Me as long as it is day; night is coming when no one can work." (John 9:3-4)* For about a half hour, I felt helpless in the darkness; a half hour followed by the tremendous joy of light.

I was given an example of what it means to work while it is day, because the night will come when we cannot work. What a message! *"For judgment I came into this world, so that those who do not see may see, and that those who see may become blind." (John 9:39)*

Not all men see, even if their eyes are physically open, according to Scripture. We can be spiritually blind because we do not know the truth. Scripture is very clear about the way that leads to Heaven. *"Truly, truly, I say to you, he who does not enter by the door into the fold of the sheep, but climbs up some other way, he is a thief and a robber." (John 10:1)* This is a truth unfolded: Not all roads or religions lead to Heaven. Not everyone sees. There is only One Way! That may come as a surprise to many who read this book, but Jesus said: *"I am the door; if anyone enters through Me, he will be saved, and will go in and out and find pasture." (John 10:9)* Laughter does not bring a sense of guilt; it brings a sense of release. It is a gift of God.

If you read the first few verses in the first chapter of James in the Bible, you will soon discover that joy should be our companion even in the midst of adversities. *"Consider it all joy, my brethren, when you encounter various trials, knowing that the testing of your faith produces endurance." (James 1:2, 3)* From that I conclude: It only hurts when we don't laugh, when we don't have our minds stayed on Him. If we are to have joy "in" trials, doesn't it stand to reason that we should have joy when we are "not" going through times of trial and testing? We should be smiling from pierced ear to pierced ear, and sideburn to sideburn, when all is well with our soul, and yet, some people look like they have just been pierced through by an arrow.

I love what the Apostle Paul shared in one of his letters to the Corinthians. He said: *". . . I determined this for my own sake, that I would not come to you in sorrow again. For if I cause you sorrow, who then makes me glad but the one whom I made sorrowful? This is the very thing I wrote you, so that when I came, I would not have sorrow from those who ought to make me rejoice; having confidence in you all that my joy would be the joy of you all." (II Corinthians 2:1-3)*

I think what Paul was pointing out is this: If he planned a trip to Corinth he wanted to go there to bring joy, and to receive joy.

As tongue twisting as my paraphrasing may sound, I believe Paul needed encouraging too, but he points out that it would not be possible for him to receive joy if he arrived and made those who should be providing joy to him, sorrowful. Paul had many afflictions and had shed many tears, and he did so while writing to the church at Corinth, and he decided that when he would visit them again, it would not be to bring sorrow but to bring joy and to receive joy. Is that a lesson for us, or what? When you go out, do you carry with you a sack of sorrow or a bushel of joy? How can you possibly reap joy when all you've sown is sorrow? We need to heed Paul's message here.

Some things are downright contagious; do you know that? I'm convinced that, if you surround yourself with people who laugh and smile a lot, it won't be long before you catch their joy. To prove my point, but on quite a different matter, I'd like to share a dog story with you:

During one of the less selfish time periods in my life, I had a Miniature Pincher. If you know anything about that particular breed of dog, you know that it not only looks like a Standard Doberman, but it has that intimidating Doberman complex. A Miniature Pincher's average weight is about eight to nine pounds, but it barks like a one hundred and thirty-five-pound guard dog, and they have a mind of their own, or so they think. I named my Pincher "Sunny," because she would always find the smallest spot of sun on the kitchen floor and she would curl up in that spot until it would move, and then she would move along with it.

Our neighbors had a male dog of no special breed whatsoever. Often, we would walk our dogs together—a morning ladies' exercise class—we liked calling it. On those walks, our dogs would do what all dogs do. On those occasions, my little Sunny would always squat, befitting her female instincts, and my friend's dog would lift his leg, befitting his male instincts. After about a month of walking our dogs together, Sunny became confused. Before long, she began to lift her leg just like her male counterpart. But she just couldn't get it right, because, I assume, God did not make her to function like a boy dog. Instead, she would back up to a tree, climb the tree with her two back legs until she was standing on her head, and then . . . yep, you guessed it; she needed a bath every time we returned from our walk. It was embarrassing for me, and if Sunny had known any better, she would have been embarrassed too. People would stop and stare, trying to figure out why in the world this small dog was doing a headstand and it was usually followed by shameless laughter. I am sure that many onlookers thought it was a trick I had taught her, since it was so out of character for a female dog to perform such an aerobic stance in order to do what she had to do. Even the neighbor's dog cocked his head, puzzled at Sunny's unnatural maneuver. Now ain't that funny!

Does anyone spend time observing you, because you are emulating Christ, even at the expense of looking strange in the eyes of the world? *"Be imitators of me, just as I also am of Christ,"* said the Apostle Paul. *(I Corinthians 11:1)* And in Ephesians 5:1, 2 we read: *". . . be imitators of God, as beloved children; walk in love, just as Christ also loved you and gave Himself up for us, an offering and a sacrifice to God as a fragrant aroma."*

Do you sometimes find yourself imitating the world, instead of Christ? Is there anything desirous about "you" that others should emulate? Oh, now there's a switch.

I knew a woman who told me, that every time she went shopping and showed her shopping treasures (or Mr. Goodbuy's, as she liked calling them) to a close friend, hardly a week passed that her friend didn't go out and buy the same thing, and usually in the same color. She told me: "We looked like the Bobsy-Twins everywhere we went together." She said that it reminded her of when she first started dating her husband. They would shop and buy matching jackets, sweaters, sunglasses, and shirts, until finally, she lost her identity.

As believers, our identity is in Christ. Aren't you glad!

Recently, I visited a friend who has a fundraising business. You know, all those students "in" and "out" of your neighborhood who knock on your door taking orders for candy, coffee, pizza, wrapping paper, nuts and popcorn? You know what I'm talking about, I'm sure. Besides her fundraising business, she also has a Bistro fetish. I have come to suspect that Guy Buffet (the Parisian designer) is a silent resident in her townhouse. From Guy Buffet paintings on her walls (her idea of wallpaper), to sets of dishes, glasses, napkins, nightlights and cheese spreaders, there's room for little else. If it were not for the hallway, cupboard and bureau tops on which photos of her children and grandchildren are displayed, the grandchildren would probably send a hit man after Guy Buffet.

Each beautifully decorated room and table is arranged for company, even though she's not expecting any. Now ain't that funny! That means, when I arrive at her home, we are relegated to a small kitchen table, which is set with Guy Buffet placemats, salt and pepper shakers and napkins you aren't allowed to use.

During my most recent visit, the purpose of which was to spend time with my friend and to accompany her on her lovely Pontoon Boat for the weekend, she said to me, "You know what, Veda, I have a lovely townhouse. It is decorated so nicely, but I rarely use any of it. Now and then I take a tour of my own house just to admire how nice it is!" With that, I broke out in uncontrollable laughter. She has a nice little television set in the kitchen, and a refrigerator full of food she never eats—samples of the things students will be selling at your door as soon as school opens. That's where we spend most of our time, unless as political co-hearts, we are watching the politically neutral Fox News Channel. When we dine, we use paper towels—to which she quickly adds—"I love paper towels!" *With a thousand Guy Buffet napkins staring you in the face*, I thought, *how could you love paper towels? You have a cemented relationship with Guy Buffet who makes lovely napkins.* "Yes, I love them too!" I reply. But it sure does provide entertainment, and I wouldn't exchange those humorous moments for anything, and I love her just the way she is.

Watching that same friend trying to find the chicken salad for our midday boating picnic lunch is enough to split a side of beef. It's impossible! As I roll in the kitchen aisle, my affection for her grows. She is uninhibited. There isn't an ounce of façade in her personality. She is just a warm and wonderful hostess and friend, albeit, she goes to bed much too early; I figure she gets tired from the lake breezes and being captain of her ship. What fun we have!

If we can't catch fish, I was thinking, as we cut a path through the water on Raystown Lake, *and we can't find the chicken salad, surely we can catch the joy, the laughter and the fun that God provides every day.*

Have you lost your joy? Just as a sheep and a coin were lost and found, because the owners searched for them, as told in two parables by Jesus, in the book of Luke, we too must look for the lost joy in our lives until we find it. In the parables, of course, Jesus is referring to seeking after the lost sinner and then experiencing great joy when he is found. If you have been seeking joy, it can be found—**IN JESUS.** You enter His joy when you become a child of His. Does this mean you go around looking like one of those canary-yellow smiley faces all the time? I don't think so. But it's imperative that we reclaim or have our joy restored, otherwise, we are a people most miserable. The best way to have joy restored, as far as I can tell, according to Scripture, is to live an obedient life in accordance with the Word of God, through confession of our sins to Him, and then by accepting the forgiveness that is wholly ours because of who Jesus is, and because of what He did for us on the Calvary Cross.

"But seek first His kingdom and His righteousness, and all these things will be added to you." (Matthew 6:33) What things will be added to you? Certainly, it does not mean by seeking His kingdom and His righteousness you will add an extra ten pounds to your weight (and aren't you glad of that!), but we will gain a peace that passes all understanding. We will not strive to thrive. In the verses previous to 6:33, we are told not to worry about what we eat, what we drink, nor what we put on. We are assured in verse 32 that our heavenly Father knows what things we need. If we settle on that—making Him our foundation, our Provider and our Rescuer, we've got a jump-start on joy!

An unknown author once said, "There is no danger of developing eyestrain from looking on the bright side."

Joy will empower you to dwell on today, put yesterday in the hands of the Lord, and begin trusting God for your future. There is where your source of joy and contentment are found.

Pick up the rod of faith, cast all your cares upon Him, and catch the laughter, catch the fun and catch the joy!

CHAPTER EIGHT

A Song in the Night

🦋 *Laurette Connelly* 🦋

There is much truth to the old adage that when you laugh, the world laughs with you. If you doubt that, try laughing out loud in a public place sometime and see how many virtual strangers begin to laugh right along with you. They have no idea what kind of silliness brought on your case of hysterics, but you have inadvertently become the cause of their impromptu laughter. You have given them a gift of respite from the doldrums of everyday living. They are not laughing *at you*, but they are drawn into the fun with you. Everyone enjoys being near someone who will make him or her laugh. There's nothing unholy about it. So lighten up! If possible throw away the pills, the antacids and laugh away the blues and the ulcers. Laughing is fun and it's catchy!

We catch enough nasty stuff from one another like colds, infections, viruses and even bad moods or bad habits. How much more pleasant to catch something that makes us relax and feel good. Catch the fun, catch the laughter and catch the joy!

Children who grow up with laughter in the home will naturally reflect that attitude in their behavior. They won't take themselves too seriously and will learn to bounce through situations that might send a more sober, stoic person into a sometimes life-long *'Pity Party Panic'* attitude.

I grew up in a home that would probably be labeled today as a dysfunctional family.

Woonsocket, Rhode Island, was composed primarily of French-speaking people who had migrated from Quebec and Montreal, Canada, before the first World War. Most came to find work in the many textile mills and to find a better way of life in the *'Land of Opportunity.'*

The French-speaking, Roman Catholic immigrants had a motto *"Dieu et la Patrie"* (God and Country). Their faith was deeply rooted in the Roman Catholic Church, their cultural identity, and the French language.

While new churches were springing up everywhere at the turn of the century, another common sight began to infiltrate the city. Though prohibition was still the law of the land, there was no shortage of underground saloons, and bootlegging was a thriving business.

When prohibition ended, saloons with swinging doors where some passed in and others passed out, became the norm in every neighborhood and a thorn in the side of housewives and mothers. Before long saloons outnumbered the huge, spired, Cathedral-style churches.

When harried housewives called in search of a wandering husband who was known to frequently have his nose in the beer behind those swingin' doors, friendly bartenders were carefully trained to say; "He hasn't been here," "Butch? Butch who? I don't know anyone by that name," or "Sam? He just left, he just dropped by to see someone, didn't stay but a minute." At the same time, he was making wild motions to Butch or Sam to pop a wintergreen mint in his mouth and make a beeline for home.

Woonsocket was not an ordinary place, not by a longshot, but it was home to me, and, in my ignorance, I assumed that it was like every other place in America.

The American dream became a foggy delusion in the hardships of the great depression. Hardly a family was left unscathed. Everywhere you looked were signs posted "NO HELP WANTED."

Husbands and fathers began to walk around neighborhoods, knocking on doors, looking for odd jobs. But who could pay for anything? The Levesque family, like most of our neighbors, joined the ranks of the 'poor.'

Papa was forced to go to the Welfare Department and sign up for relief. We were given a pass to get free food consisting of potatoes, flour, dried peas, and dried prunes. Our shoes were lined with thick cardboard to fill the gaping holes in the soles so we wouldn't burn our feet on the hot pavement in the summer.

When things at home went from bad to worse and finances couldn't be stretched any further, the family continually moved from one small apartment to another. Always having to downsize until eventually nine of us lived in a small four-room tenement with no shower, no bath and no hot water. The apartment was in an eight family house, adjacent to the local fire station and across from a textile factory.

It was a sad and challenging time for most adults as they struggled to make ends meet and keep a hold on dignity. But most of us children didn't really know how desperately poor we were because everyone we knew lived the same way we did. We all stood in line for food and we all wore government-donated clothing.

The word vacation meant only that school was out for the summer. We never expected to go anywhere. Summertime meant we could walk around barefoot, play outdoors in the rain and jump in puddles or walk to the local park. We could take spoons and go to the back of the ice cream parlor where they threw away the empties. After shooing the flies away, we practically fell into the very tall containers head-first trying to reach the leftover unscooped ice cream at the bottom. On a good day, we could find several different flavors, maybe even my favorite . . . pistachio.

Every morning we could watch the firemen practice how to rescue someone from a make-believe fire. All the kids in the neighborhood tried to make it sound more authentic for them by coughing and yelling, "Help! Fireman, fireman! I'm burning! . . . cough . . . cough . . . Save my baby!" We had a ringside seat once a month when they jumped into a net from the third, fourth or fifth floor of a brick practice tower that faced our backyard. What child could want for anything more? We had everything we needed to keep us happy but we also had parents riddled with fears; parents who were not easily amused or contented.

To try to retain their sanity and keep themselves from slipping into personal, chronic depression, adults made their own fun, they got together to play cards or board games. Often in the steamy heat of summer nights when electric fans were too expensive to run and there was no way to keep cool in the unbearably hot apartments, the neighbors would gather in the large, cement, fenced-in yard. They would sit and talk for hours about old times or recount favorite, mystery stories conceived in the depths of their own imaginations. They were master storytellers who clearly tried to outdo one another with the most chilling of sound effects. You could almost see the creaking doors "*screeeech,*" feel the warmth of flowing blood and hear shrieking sounds "*Aaaagh!*" as they spun their terrifying tales. It was the stuff that nightmares were made of. Naive, wide-eyed children hung onto every word, innocently believing as absolute truth the authenticity of the spine-tingling stories.

Often, on Friday evenings, the firemen next door would come into our large yard leaving one fireman behind to hear the alarm in case an emergency should arise. All the residents of the eight family house would carry out lanterns and kitchen chairs to form a wide circle in the yard. Young mothers took out large wicker baby carriages and sat fanning themselves with cardboard fans while lulling the babies to sleep. Others filled a couple of large galvanized tubs with water for little ones to splash and play in to keep cool. Fathers spread a blanket on the ground and made a tent with another blanket thrown over a clothesline for kids who might get sleepy. A barrel was set on its side with a large plank balancing in the center to serve as a seesaw for older kids. Little boys ran around chasing squealing little girls who pretended they didn't want to be the object of their attention. Younger children preferred to chase fireflies, trapping them in covered glass jars. It was a scene that might have come straight out of the mind of a young Norman Rockwell.

Meek Mr. Charette, on the third floor, could make incredible music with nothing but a couple of kitchen spoons. Mr. Lemoine, who lived with his wife and seven children on the second floor, could make a washboard sound like a base fiddle. Mr. Duprée played the harmonica and my father played the fiddle. Granted they were not the "Boston Pops" but they were all we had. They were loud, they were available and we appreciated them.

Before we knew it, other neighbors on the street began to drift in with little ones in tow when they heard the unmistakable call of the familiar foot stomping music. *"Swing your partner, hi and low. Now grab the next, don't let her go—all sweet lassies take a bow, laddies can't, they don't know how! Yee-Haw!"* That was an open invitation for anyone to come and join in a good old-fashioned Hoe Down that went on until the cool night air made sleeping in the hot tenements more tolerable.

We never got through a Hoe Down without at least one long drawn out round of *"Alouette, Gentille Allouette"* starting from the Alouette's beak to its little feet. Flossie, a heavy-set maiden lady in her fifties, was always the first to arrive in her dowdy cotton housedress covered up with a full apron, rolled down bobbie sox and scuffed up brown-lace shoes. She sat most of the evening with a frozen smile on her face, now and then stuffing a pinch of *"chickaberry snuff"* up her nose. Everyone knew the party would not end until Flossie graced us with her warbling rendition of, *"I Won't Dance, Don't Ask Me."* The children who were still awake, would wince and block their ears in anticipation of her last high pitched note which was an official call for parents to gather their offspring together and say goodnight.

Those cheerful summer evenings saw us through many tough years. In spite of widespread poverty, there was laughter. Laughter was the prescription for healthy living in the midst of wilderness times. *I wonder if Moses and the Israelites gathered around their tents for an occasional evening of fun and storytelling in the dry heat of the desert?*

Neighbors who had become chronic complainers found few sympathizers willing to give ear to their unhappy, negative tirades. If they chose to weep in their home-brew or in their tea, they wept alone. Others counted their blessings and made the best of unpleasant circumstances. Before the saying was popular, they knew how to make sweet tasting lemonade when they'd been handed nothing but sour lemons.

Still, the "Joy of the Lord" was a foreign concept to most people. They laughed and made their fun because if they didn't they would drown in the heavy torrent of troubled waters. And so, the saloons flourished. It was not the spirit of God that gave the men comfort, but the spirits found in unpromising bottles. Even so, people did learn to laugh and others laughed with them. Laughter brought relief, it made the bleak depression years more tolerable. It also prepared them for future disappointments and trials.

Sometimes we don't like where God has led us. Our lives are not on the course we had mapped out for ourselves. *"You know Lord, I always wanted to have two children three years apart and be a stay-at-home mom. But you sent me very lively twins when my oldest child was only two and now here I am pregnant again. That was not part of my plan. Did you mean to do that? My husband and I spent a small fortune decorating our home so that it looks like a Martha Stewart creation, and now we live with wall to wall 'Cheerios.' There's always a teddy bear, a rubber duck or something floating in the toilet. The puppy you sent us weighs sixty-five pounds and flunked obedience school three times. Lord, I graduated 'Cum Laude' with a degree in merchandising. That was no small feat. (By the way, I haven't seen my feet in four years.) All I ever do is change messy diapers and blow runny noses! Why didn't someone tell me that two year olds, like Houdini, could climb out of anyplace if they put their minds to it. This is not what I expected when I said 'I do.'"*

Yet, God doesn't seem to want to change things and you want to yell; *"God, why don't You do something? Why don't You answer my prayers? Don't You care that I'm not happy?"*

I wonder if God ever feels like saying; *"My child, have you ever considered having friends over for a Hoe Down?"*

God does answer our prayers but He doesn't always change our circumstances. What He changes is our attitude. His goal for us is not our happiness in this brief, fragile, temporary world. He has a much more lofty and lasting goal in mind for His children. His purpose for our lives is that we should attain *eternal* happiness and spend eternity with Him in His kingdom. In the meantime, there's work to be done. We are to be His witnesses.

"You shall receive power when the Holy Spirit has come upon you; and you shall be My witnesses both in Jerusalem, and in all Judea and Samaria, and even to the remotest part of the earth." (Acts 1:8)

"Therefore we do not lose heart, but though our outer man is decaying, yet our inner man is being renewed day by day, for momentary, light affliction is producing for us an eternal weight of glory far beyond all comparison." (2 Corinthians 4:16, 17)

"I have told you these things, so that in me you may have peace. In this world you will have trouble. But take heart! I have overcome the world." (John 16:33)

The Apostle Paul suffered a shipwreck, beatings, stoning, and he endured them all with incredible perseverance. But there was one thing he wanted very much to have changed. It may have been a problem that caused him to be disfigured. Whatever it was, he found it difficult to live with and he did ask God to remove it from him on a number of occasions, but God said "No." He doesn't always answer with a "Yes."

"To keep me from becoming conceited because of these surpassingly great revelations, there was given me a thorn in my flesh, a messenger of Satan, to torment me. Three times I pleaded with the Lord to take it away from me. But He said to me, 'My grace is sufficient for you, for my power is made perfect in weakness.'" (II Corinthians 12: 7-9)

Paul's situation didn't change but his attitude did. His response was one of acceptance: "Therefore I will boast all the more gladly about my weaknesses, so that Christ's power may rest on me."

Paul understood the "Joy of the Lord." He wasn't looking for the *"Good Life"* on this earth. He'd had a taste of that kind of life before he got a taste of Jesus. Paul was a highly educated Jew and Roman citizen who had studied under the most respected teacher and Rabbi, Gamaliel. He himself had gained great respect as a strong Pharisaical leader. But Paul never doubted that even with the thorn in his flesh, even with all the hardships and trials he had to suffer as an Apostle of Jesus Christ, following Jesus was sweeter and more promising than anything he'd ever known. Though he suffered incredible persecution and he was stripped of all dignity, no one could strip him of the joy he had in the knowledge and love of Jesus.

Paul knew the freedom he had in Jesus was a freedom that extended far beyond the Roman shackles that had him bound hand and foot.

"The crowd joined in the attack against Paul and Silas, and the magistrates ordered them to be stripped and beaten. After they had been severely flogged, they were thrown into prison, and the jailer was commanded to guard them carefully. Upon receiving such orders, he put them in the inner cell and fastened their feet in the stocks. About midnight Paul and Silas were praying and singing hymns to God, and the other prisoners were listening to them." (Acts 16:22-25)

When we're agonizing over something, the midnight hour is usually when things seem darkest and hope gives way to despair. We're not in the mood to have a *"Gospel concert"* but His Word tells us that God gives us songs in the night.

"The Lord will command His loving kindness in the daytime; And His song will be with me in the night, A prayer to the God of my life." (Psalm 42:8)

"But no one says, 'Where is God my Maker, who gives songs in the night.'" (Job 35:10)

Charles Hadddon Spurgeon said: "Any fool can sing in the day. It's easy to sing when we can read the notes by daylight; but the skillful singer is he who can sing when there's not a ray of light to read by."

Paul and Silas were given songs in the night in the depths of the darkest dungeon. If they had any kind of an attitude, it was one of tremendous hope for that glorious morning when they would sing the song of Victory in Jesus as they stood in His awesome presence. They could not be robbed of the joy of the Lord!

"Now is your time of grief, but I will see you again and you will rejoice, and no-one will take away your joy." (John 16:22)

Laughter and joy are not inseparable. A person can have laughter but be totally lacking in joy. You need only to watch a few of the appalling talk shows on television today. They somehow survive by exploiting troubled people who will do or say anything for a free trip to the big city sending the callous audience into foolish, raucous laughter. Ironically, even that kind of laughter probably still has some therapeutic value because it's a release, but it's totally unrelated to "Joy." Laughter is good, but joy goes deeper than laughter.

Happiness and joy are not inseparable. One can have happiness and not have a trace of joy. Happiness is circumstantial, when all is going well, when the stock market is skyrocketing, your job is prospering, when the family is healthy and the children prefer good grades to green hair and pierced tongues, you can be happy. But, when the bottom falls out of the market, when the company you work for has downsized and you're the first to be let go, when the children think they and all their friends are budding Einsteins, and, you might as well be illiterate because you know nothing, then, happiness can be very elusive.

Have you ever watched dedicated (fanatic) fans when their favorite football team has made it to the Super Bowl? If their team wins, they're ecstatic. Grown men pour buckets of juice or bottles of champagne over each other's heads. Everyone gets caught up in the excitement. They ring noisy cowbells, blow whistles and shoot off fireworks. They dance and cheer, throw confetti everywhere and drive through towns leaning on car horns. Some will celebrate by consuming all the alcohol they can get their hands on. These fans would say they're *happy* but that happiness is short-lived when the team's victory becomes only a memory or the hangover kicks in after hours of drunken celebration. When the state team loses, where are the fans?

Joy goes deeper than happiness. The Joy of the Lord reaches into your very soul to give you an indescribable peace at the realization that even in the deepest of pits, you are not alone, He is there to comfort. He'll walk through the fire with you just as He did with Meshack, Shadrack, and Abednago.

"The Lord is my shepherd, I shall not be in want. He makes me lie down in green pastures, He leads me beside quiet waters, He restores my soul. He guides me in paths of righteousness for His name's sake. Even though I walk through the valley of the shadow of death, I will fear no evil, for you are with me; your rod and your staff, they comfort me." (Psalm 23:1-4)

"Be strong and courageous. Do not be afraid or terrified because of them, for the Lord your God goes with you; He will never leave you nor forsake you." (Deuteronomy 31:6)

"If God is for us, who is against us?" (Romans 8:31)

If God is *with* us and *for* us, restoring us, guiding and comforting us, is there a battle that can't be won or a problem that can't be solved? Yes . . . if we keep our eyes on the burdens that weigh us down rather than on the One who has offered to carry them with us. Believers sometimes forget to whom they have entrusted their lives. They feel alone when He's only inches away with His hand extended to help them.

"Come to me, all you who are weary and burdened, and I will give you rest. Take my yoke upon you and learn from me, for I am gentle and humble in heart, and you will find rest for your souls. For my yoke is easy and my burden is light." (Matthew 11:28-30)

> The first step is to Come. Come to Him–
> Then we're to Take. Take His yoke.
> In other words, become joined with Him–
> Then we will Find. Find rest for our souls.

As soon as we deliver our burdens to the foot of the cross, we immediately feel the relief of a helping hand. If we try to carry them ourselves, we're likely to develop a hernia from the sheer weight of them. Life becomes more simple and joyful when we are one with Him.

Laughter and happiness are not always brought on by joy, they sometimes stand alone, but apart from "joy" they can be volatile and undependable. Emotions can plummet from an all-time *"high"* to an all-time *"low"* at any encounter with disappointment. But the "Joy of the Lord" is the solid foundation for lasting happiness and easy laughter even in the midst of turmoil. The "Joy of the Lord" encompasses laughter and happiness together and brings it to completion and contentment for everyday living.

"I am coming to you now, but I saw these things while I am still in the world, so that they may have the full measure of my joy within them." (John 17:13)

CHAPTER NINE

The Staying Power of Joy

🐝 *Veda Boyd* 🐝

> *"Tis easy enough to be pleasant,*
> *Then life flows along like a song;*
> *But the man (woman) worthwhile is the one who will smile*
> *When everything goes dead wrong."*
> *- Ella Wheeler (1855-1919)*

A long time ago, I discovered the difference between happiness and joy, two of the most interchangeable words in the English language. The core difference, in my humble opinion, is based more on the source of one's joy and happiness, rather than on its expression.

The true meaning of joy and its sidekick, happiness, has been so trivialized by current new-age philosophies and false religion that sometimes it's hard to tell the difference between the two.

Sitting on my sand chair, deep enough in the water's edge to feel the ocean waves crashing over my legs—each wave breaking at the right time and within its boundary—what joy comes to my heart! I marvel at God, the Creator, and His magnificent and perfect plan for the waters of the earth.

Looking out across the vastness of an ocean deeper and bluer than Paul Newman's eyes (proof that I'm still alive), I think, *if God cares enough for the things of creation—enough to stop the waters from consuming the whole earth, stopping it just short enough for one of His created beings to enjoy sitting only feet away from the immeasurable depth of His ocean, without having it spill over me, how much more does He care for me*! It's not the only time, but whenever I head for the beaches of North Carolina and Maryland, that truth renews itself to me.

What God reveals to me through His creation, He also confirms with verses from Psalm 74:13-17), *"You divided the sea by Your strength; You broke the heads of the sea monsters in the waters. You crushed the heads of Leviathan; You gave him as food for the creatures of the wilderness. You broke open springs and torrents; You dried up every-flowing stream. Yours is the day, Yours also is the night; You have prepared the light and the sun. You have established all the boundaries of the earth; You have made summer and winter."*

What greater example of the boundary setter's handiwork could He have given us than the place where the ocean meets the shore? As part of God's creation, we have tried time after time to make our own boundaries, breaking His. We allow sin to rush into our lives like the waves on the shore. When we choose poorly, letting sin in, our joy is often lost, washed out to sea. If the source of our joy is earthly pleasures, it's a momentary delight. True joy has staying power!

When I read these words in the book of Hebrews, it seems clear that sin is one of the culprits that restricts our joy: *". . . since we have so great a cloud of witnesses surrounding us, let us also lay aside every encumbrance, and the sin which so easily entangles us, and let us run with endurance the race that is set before us, fixing our eyes on Jesus, the author and perfecter of our faith, who for the joy set before Him endured the cross, despising the shame, and has sat down at the right hand of the throne of God. For consider Him who has endured such hostility by sinners against Himself, so that you may not grow weary and lose heart." (Hebrews 12:1-3)* Jesus has made a way for us to not grow weary and lose heart. Did you get that? The joy of the Lord is in our corner, He took the brunt of our sin, so why do you look like you just suffered a "technical knock out" in the ring of life?

As far as I can tell, from reading God's Word: Land, sea, sky and I belong to Him. And this Very God offers us eternal life. I find that awesome! It brings joy, comfort and confidence to my heart as I apply it to my life.

"And they who dwell in the ends of the earth stand in awe of Thy signs; You who makes the dawn and the sunset shout for joy." (Psalm 65:8) *"The meadows are clothed with flocks, And the valleys are covered with grain; They shout for joy, yes, they sing."* (Psalm 65:13). *"Let the field exalt, and all that is in it. Then all the trees of the forest will sing for joy."* (Psalm 96:12). *"Let the rivers clap their hands; Let the mountains sing together for joy."* (Psalm 98:8). *"When I consider Your heavens, the work of Your fingers, The moon and the stars, which You have ordained . . . "* (Psalm 8:3)

Do you have a personal relationship with the Creator?

Joy in knowing Jesus produces optimism. However, to quote Oswald Chambers, "Optimism, apart from a man's belief and his acceptance of Christianity, may be healthy-minded, but it is blinded; when he faces the facts of life as they are, uncolored by his temperament, despair is the only possible ending for him."

As Christians, if we walk with the Lord, our cup runneth over! We should be on a continuous joy ride through life. If not externally evident by broad smiles and laughter, it should be internally manifested in our attitudes and dispositions regarding every circumstance. I am convinced, however, that laughter is God's way of touching our lives and our egregious world with His loving hand.

If you are miserable today, you have undoubtedly escaped the hand of our caring Lord, not by His choice, but by your own. The question must be asked: What is the source of your unhappiness, your lack of joy?

The greatest joy I know is the assurance that God has forgiven me of all my sins, past, present and future and that when I became a child of His, it was forever. That's a dose of WOW JOY! I am so happy that my salvation (faith in God's Only Son and His shed blood for me) is not a fleeting position, but one that has staying power—forever power, by His grace alone.

Does that mean I will never experience hardships and disappointments? Of course not! There will be all kinds of everyday annoyances that are upsetting (joy-killers, if you will), that have nothing to do with the joy of my salvation. I've often said I know it's going to be a good day for me when all four wheels of my grocery cart are going in the same direction. But even when I get a cart that resembles an automobile with bad shocks and two flat tires (joy-killer), it brings a smile to my face, especially as I try to maneuver the cart into the cart-stall without hitting fellow shoppers and their vehicles. As I was ramming my grocery cart into the tail-end of the row of carts at the "cart station" one day (an opportunity for me to vent my frustration over a guy that had earlier turned in front of me and robbed me of my parking space), I saw a Christian fish symbol on the back of a pre-pre-pre-owned vehicle in the parking lot. Instead of the letters spelling Jesus on the inside of the fish, it spelled out Satan. I knew that that person was going to have a bad life and death, if things besides her fish emblem didn't change. I took a moment and prayed for that misled lost soul. It was one of those times I could not laugh.

It is possible to maintain an attitude of joy during weighty trials—when the news is not what we expect or what we want to hear. We can also be joyful when facing all those daily miniscule annoyances. You see, no man and no circumstance can rob us of the joy God places inside of us. The joy of the Lord has staying power!

What you may have faced, or may be facing, may not bring you happiness, but if you are a Christian, the joy of the Lord will sustain and keep you through those trials. That is the difference between the staying power of joy and short-lived happiness. Happiness will elude you in times of trouble, but God will never leave or forsake you, and if He is there with you, so is the joy that is found in Him. *". . . I will never desert you, nor will I ever forsake you . . ." (Hebrews 13:5)* There's the real source of our joy!

If we are truthful, we will have to acknowledge that it's the external circumstances in our lives that affect our happiness. Doesn't your happiness often depend on other people and things? Ok, I'll go first; I'll be honest. I am just the happiest person in the world when I am with people fatter than I am. Compliments make me happy. I'm happy when I'm cracking hard-shell crabs with a wooden mallet and imagining the crab to be some unsuspecting foe. I'm happy when my boss gives me a raise. I'm happy when I get a chapter of a book written with less than one hundred errors because other people haven't demanded my attention. I'm happy if, at my age, I get a second look instead of a terrorist threat. Which reminds me: I read recently that the Israelis told jokes and made each other laugh when being bombarded by scud-missiles during the Gulf War. At the time, they couldn't strike back in response to a plea from the United States to withhold retaliation, the article claimed, and the only way to retain some semblance of normality was to tell stories and laugh. In the midst of trials, they may have laughed, but I believe it was their deep faith in God and His plan for their nation and people that evidenced joy in the midst of war, an internal joy that went deeper than external laughter.

The reason I feel comfortable in repeating that story is because of a letter I personally received from the Advisor to then Prime Minister Yitzhak Shamir during the Gulf War, in response to a letter of encouragement I had sent to him that included a promise to pray for the nation of Israel. The hand-addressed letter came to me dated February 19, 1991 and was marked: Prime Minister's Bureau, Jerusalem:

> "Dear Mrs. Boyd
>
> I am writing on behalf of the Prime Minister, Mr. Yitzhak Shamir, to acknowledge your letter, and to thank you for your warm sentiments, which are a source of encouragement in these trying days.
>
> In this struggle against the forces of evil, we draw strength and comfort from the immortal words in Psalm 121:
>
> 'The Guardian of Israel shall neither slumber nor sleep.'
>
> Shalom, from Jerusalem
> A.H. Hurwitz, Advisor to the Prime Minister"

Needless to say, I have cherished that response. Mostly, I share in worshiping the Guardian of Israel. Joy goes deep when it has its foundation in faith in the God of Abraham, Isaac, and Jacob. For me personally, it goes a step deeper. I believe in God's Son, Jesus, and in the Holy Spirit, the Comforter whom Jesus gave us, and who resides within every believer. *"As I live, says the Lord, every knee shall bow to*

Me and every tongue shall give praise to God. So then, each one of us will give an account of himself to God." (Romans 14:11, 12) There is no getting around it; every tongue will confess that Jesus Christ is Lord. If you don't confess it now, you'll get your chance. That's a God given guarantee, according to the Word of God. The Scripture says we will confess, but it also says that our opportunity to trust Christ as our Savior comes to us on this side of death. *". . . Behold, now is The Acceptable Time, behold, now is The Day of Salvation." (II Corinthians 6:2)* So, what are you waiting for?

The late great and godly man, Dwight L. Moody put it this way: "Happiness is caused by things that happen around me, and circumstances will mar it; but joy flows right on through trouble; joy flows on through the dark; joy flows in the night as well as in the day; joy flows all through persecution and opposition. It is an unceasing fountain bubbling up in the heart; a secret spring the world can't see and doesn't know anything about. The Lord gives his people perpetual joy when we walk in obedience to Him."

When you understand the difference between joy and happiness, you should begin to desire the best: JOY! True joy, found in the person of Jesus, helps all of us to face our circumstances with a different attitude, even though there may be tears in our eyes and a deep ache in our hearts, because our minds are stayed on HIM. *"The steadfast of mind You will keep in perfect peace, because He trusts in You." (Isaiah 26:3)* But I must be clear here: If you have never made a decision to trust Jesus Christ as your Savior, then you do not possess real joy and you have settled, at least until now, for superficial happiness that depends on circumstances and other people. I personally settled for superficial joy for many years.

True joy comes from within and is evidenced by how we live, act, and react, outwardly. Happiness is temporary; it comes and goes like a weekly paycheck. Joy that comes from a personal relationship with Jesus has STAYING POWER!

What do you suppose keeps you from experiencing joy?

If you are anything like me, your mind is set on things temporal—more than you'd like to admit—and certainly more than I would like to admit. I think a lot about chocolate, and more often, about hot fudge. When I fast, "slowly," and give up that luscious dark gooey substance, which necessitates tying my hands behind my back and taping my mouth shut, I complain that joy has gone out of my life. But that's a lie. My joy is still there; it's my mind that has refocused on temporal gratification. Perhaps that is why diets based on Biblical principals are such a success these days. I can't help wondering if "Thou shalt not eat hot fudge" had been one of the Ten Commandments, it would have made any difference in my eating habits. I'm so glad Moses wasn't told to write that one down! But isn't it true? We have these preconceived ideas of what will bring us joy, when really all we are trying to do is feel momentarily happy. Oh, that word "feel," it gives me the willies. If anything can mess up our minds and choices, it's that worldly advice: Do it if it feels good. Hot fudge makes me happy, but it also makes me fat! A whole lot of the time, what makes us happy are things that are not necessarily good for us. But joy, ah-h-h, real joy, that will still be there when all the stores have run out of hot fudge. *". . . the mind set on the Spirit is life and peace." (Romans 8:6)* And where there is life and peace, there is JOY! In the midst of war (and a shortage of hot fudge), there can be peace and inner joy.

To have a joy-filled life—joy for all seasons—it takes putting first things first. That would be a personal relationship with Jesus. From there, it's like coming back to home base after a home run, or a strike out, knowing that the One who loves at all times is there waiting for you. The difference again is the source. Jesus loves unconditionally, unlike fickle sports fans that will cheer for you one minute and throw insults at you the next.

As Christians, laughter is a byproduct of inner joy. So why aren't you laughing, or at the very least, smiling?

Ultimately, even when facing death, Jesus knew that the reward waiting for Him would be joy, because of His obedience to His Father. How simple that sounds to us, we who did not have to pay a single cent for the sins of the world, let alone, give our very life. I believe one of the many joys set before Jesus was the salvation of the people who would come to believe in Him and who would turn from sin and enter into the joy of the Lord.

The staying power of Joy is very important in our walk with Jesus.

Look around you. Evidently, many Christians are stuck on stoic, or problems they don't have, but are trying hard to get. Are they Christians? Yes, if they believe in Jesus and have repented of their sins. Why then do many Christians appear joyless?

When anyone trusts in Christ, the Holy Spirit comes to dwell in him, a person who convicts the new creature in Christ, of sin. Because he is a new creature he now has the power through Christ to choose right over wrong. Before the indwelling of the Holy Spirit, there was no one living in him who convicted him of wrong actions and thoughts. Thus, he did what he wanted to do. The battle between right and wrong begins when Christ comes to reside in each of us. The same power that enables us to choose right over wrong, is the same power that enables us to choose staying-power-joy! It is available in every believer.

Even though the stoic Christian is still a Christian, the world needs to see the evidence of changed lives, lives that bring joy, warmth and love to those who are lost, or to fellow Christians who are hurting. Unfortunately, there are Christians who are not choosing joy, who are hiding their joy under a bushel, something I was warned about in a song I sang in Bible School when I was a little girl.

In Acts 13:52 we read that the *"disciples were continually filled with joy and with the Holy Spirit."* One: They were full of joy continually. Two: It says that they were filled with the Holy Spirit. Consider this: The fact that they were indwelled by the Holy Spirit made them joyful continually. That sounds like a group of guys who were happy inside and out. How sad that some Christians look like they've just been siphoned of every drop of joy; their lives ring hollow and they're left thirsting, and the dwelling place of the Holy Spirit begins to resemble a gloomy room on a cold foggy day.

How can you be attracted to someone who doesn't smile, who doesn't have a sense of humor, who doesn't exhibit joy? People do not have to be physically pretty or handsome for people to be attracted to them. The Bible says, *"He has no stately form or majesty, that we should look upon Him, Nor appearance that we should be at-*

tracted to Him." (Isaiah 53:2) Imagine that! Jesus probably was never mistaken for Charlton Heston during his days on earth, yet He drew crowds wherever he went. Why? His attractiveness went deeper. Besides His miracles, I believe the joy of the Father was visible in His face. I believe He laughed with children and He possessed a message of hope. He was full of compassion and He loved. All of those things drew people to Him. Are we, as Christians, drawing people to Christ because they see those same qualities in us? Or, is what we emanate attracting more bugs than people?

Have you ever played the game, "To Tell The Truth?" It's played like this: There are usually four or five contestants, and they pick something really significant that one of them has done, and the audience tries to figure out who that person is by asking a series of questions. Each panel member tries to convince the questioner that the significant action or event involved him or her. It's a lot of fun. I wonder, as we walk through life, whether or not people can tell we are the Christians.

Remember when you first fell in love? There was a glow about you and it stayed there until you were married. Just kidding (it lasts at least five years), but it didn't take long before you had to invest some painstaking effort in it to keep it going, right? Perhaps even now, you are struggling to keep your marriage together. To keep your marriage and your walk with the Lord new and exciting, you must be involved: Involved in obedience, involved in communicating, and involved in loving, as Christ loves. Now please, don't tell me you have the PERFECT marriage, because, I'll tell you that you are stretching the truth. If you are Christ-like—not too troubled, fearful or easily defeated—people are bound to ask why. The Bible says, *". . . always be ready to make a defense to everyone who asks you to give an account for the hope that is in you, yet with gentleness and reverence . . . " (I Peter 3:15)* The only reason I can think of, that anyone would ask about the hope that is in us, or why there are repaired and replenished relationships, is because Christians are different, and they are expected by others to be different. Jesus wants to reign over selfish whims and desires. If that first intimate love for Him has been maintained, it is possible to live that kind of life. But, if you allow that love to grow cold, frost will cling to every branch of your life, and soon that branch will break off, and the consequences of the separation will be felt, and you will have lost your glow.

There is an old saying, and I do believe they are even lyrics in a song: "Let a smile be your umbrella, on a rainy, rainy day." The world-view rebuttal is: "The only thing you'll get is a mouth full of water." As Christians, we are under the protective wings of our Lord, a shelter in the time of a storm. We "shall not" drown in our sorrows, even if we're swimming upstream physically and emotionally. God does not leave us endlessly floundering there. We have a rescuer! But we can refuse the lifeline. We may have storms (and we probably will), even tornadoes at times, and our lives may lean a little, or be off balance, but if we belong to God, our foundation remains strong. If that doesn't bring a smile to your face, then you're more than likely missing all your teeth, that's all I can say.

One day, when I arrived home from work, I discovered that the plumber had been there and had replaced my faucet in the bathroom, per my request. The problem was: he had forgotten to replace the middle board beneath the sink, the divider between the left and right doors of my sink cupboard, which apparently had been removed for easy access to the plumbing fixtures beneath my sink. Instead of calling him and asking him to please come back and replace that particular board, I decided I would go to the local hardware store and get a bottle of wood glue and do it myself.

Being a not-so-handy-woman, I faced my problem head-on, minus a game plan. I began squeezing the glue container . . . HARD. I thought it was going to be the consistency of Elmer's Glue. Instead, it ran out like water, and soon I had a whole container of glue all over my fingers, on the floor, and very little on the piece of wood. My fingers were now stuck together. Instead of calling 911, or the plumber, I decided to reach for the toilet tissue and wipe the glue from my hands, thinking I could just begin again. You guessed it; not only were my fingers stuck together, but now I sat there with a roll of toilet tissue attached as well. It was a sight to behold and an even bigger mess.

Instead of screaming, or calling myself names, befitting the situation, I decided to have a good laugh. Suddenly, the problem didn't seem nearly as unsolvable. With my hands completely unusable, and my body squished between the commode and the bathroom sink, I managed to retrieve a full bottle of fingernail polish remover, which also stuck to my hand. I poured the polish remover all over my hands and slowly, my fingers began to separate. To add injury to the situation, the fumes nearly knocked me out. Fortunately for me, I lost very little skin and was left with just an unsightly manicure and a wasted roll of toilet tissue.

Why would anyone be satisfied going through life being a "Gluey Gus?" Oops! I mean "Gloomy Gus?"

Joy has staying power, but we must draw daily from the well of that joy—JESUS. Not only in times of sorrow, or the "sticky" situations of life, but a continual filling, by spending time in His Word and just "hangin' out with Him," as I recently heard a speaker challenge his listeners to do.

I don't often read the Song of Solomon, but with regard to the subject of joy, I thought Solomon 4:6 was worth some consideration. *"Until the daybreak, and the shadows flee away, I will get me to the mountain of myrrh, and to the hill of frankincense."*

Are you determined to get to the mountain of joy and to the hill of frankincense? You will not need hiking boots or a backpack full of gear to reach the apex of joy. With a cruel cross on His back, Jesus took your and my sin-burdens upon His shoulders and He climbed the hill for us. It was there, on that hill, that He made the ultimate sacrifice for you and me. For His death and resurrection, He was honored by the Father, so that you and I can experience the staying power of joy.

I received an e-mail while writing this chapter that made me smile. I do not know who wrote it, but I am going to take the liberty of repeating it. I take absolutely no credit for any part of it, but I am claiming the message for my own, and perhaps you will too. It was like catching the essence of God's fondness for me. It read: "If God had a refrigerator, my picture would be on it. He'd have a photo of me in His wallet. He sends flowers to me in the spring and a sunrise every morning. I talk and He listens. He could have picked an earthly mansion in which to live, yet He chose to live in my heart." Isn't that special? It deserves a place on your refrigerator, and mine, as a reminder of how much we are loved.

For those of you who are walking around with a frown branded on your brow, be thankful you are walking, and if you are thankful you are walking, then replace that frown with a smile.

I happen to have a granddaughter who will most likely spend the rest of her life in a wheelchair. She is fourteen years old. She has not known the joy of walking, playing or running. The things we do for ourselves, without even thinking, she struggles to accomplish, after much mental and physical deliberation. She sits upright with the help of a rod in her back. She must depend on others for some of the most menial tasks, and yet, her face radiates, her eyes twinkle, and she prays and believes in the God who has not healed her body after many years of prayers by family and friends. God has a special purpose for precious Grace, even if we will never know why, on this side of heaven.

Have you ever met a perpetual complainer? They are never well, even if they look like a million bucks with rosy cheeks. I often think, when I meet people like that: *You ought to spend a day in my granddaughter's shoes.* People say to me, and quite often I might add, that if anything is going to happen or anyone is going to get something, it will happen to you and you will get it. I admit, they are not off by much when they say that. I'm the infamous Calamity Jane. Yet, because my joy is rooted in Jesus, the things that happen to me, and the things I get, will not defeat me. I may not be pain-free or immune to bad circumstances, but like my granddaughter in her wheelchair, I keep on wheeling.

You do not have to spend your life in a mental wheelchair. Search for myrrh and frankincense, from daybreak until the shadows flee away, and may that treasure of staying-power-joy be demonstrated by the curve of your mouth and the flame on your candle. LET IT SHINE, LET IT SHINE, LET IT SHINE!

CHAPTER TEN

Joyful Journey Home

✻ *Laurette Connelly* ✻

"Consider it pure joy, my brothers, whenever you face trials of many kinds."
-James 1:2

As I'm just about to begin writing this chapter on rejoicing in the Lord, my initial outline will have to be revised as I ponder the events of the last week. Just a few days ago our nation went through the first major assault we've ever seen on our own turf. Everyone sat glued to television sets in stunned disbelief as, over and over again, we saw the scene of two jumbo jets slamming into the World Trade Center in New York City. We watched in helpless horror as the Twin Towers began to crumble, trapping thousands of innocent civilians in the rubble. We cried at the sight of hundreds of people covered with hot ash, running frantically from a gigantic cloud of black smoke rushing to engulf them. Stunned businessmen and women still clutching dusty briefcases walked dazedly as if in mindless circles. The sight was like a science fiction movie. *This can't be real,* I thought, *not here, not in the land of the free and the home of the brave. Who, in their right mind, would ever want to do such a horrible thing?*

Within minutes another hijacked plane crashed into the Pentagon building in Washington, D.C., killing well over a hundred people. A third plane, apparently headed for either the Capitol or the White House, crashed in a field in Pennsylvania after heroic passengers banded together to block the evil plans of the indifferent uncaring terrorists.

In an instant, thousands of young, innocent people lost their lives in an unexpected, hateful act of terrorism and over six thousand American children were added to the roster of "one parent" families. Within days, our peaceful country was at war and threats of continuing terrorism began to plague us.

How and where does one find joy? Can anything good spring from the ashes of shattered lives? Where was God on September 11, 2001? Has He forsaken us? Rejoice in the Lord always? Is that reasonable?

Meditating on that question, I come up with only one answer that makes any sense at all—"We're not home yet, we're just not home." We live in a fallen world where there's no such thing as fairness. If fairness was a part of this world, we would not see inequality of such great proportions, where some people live in extreme poverty while others enjoy tremendous privilege. Some go through life in perfect health and others struggle through every day with incredible hardship. In this temporary place, pain is a reality and every bit of it is the result of sin. This is not the world as God meant it to be when He created the Garden. This is the world that man has polluted with his own selfish desires.

It's true that evil men can terrorize us and even have the power to kill us. But Jesus, and Jesus alone, has the power to raise us up again. Even the Koran will ascribe that power to Jesus, and Jesus alone.

God's Word, the Bible, is very clear on the subject:

"I tell you, my friends, do not be afraid of those who kill the body and after that can do no more. But I will show you whom you should fear: Fear Him who, after the killing of the body, has power to throw you into hell. Yes, I tell you, fear Him." (Luke 12:4, 5)

This world is only a shadow of our permanent home. The reality is yet to come and in that reality there will be fairness. If you see the shadow of a building, you know there has to be the reality of a building. There's no shadow without a reality. The reality of our home is the Kingdom of God. That's the believer's permanent, eternal home. The Apostle Paul tells us that our citizenship is in heaven. Believers are a heavenly people with a heavenly citizenship. With that in mind, we can have the joy of the Lord, though we see pain all around us and live in the shadow of the Twin Towers. We are a people of hope and promise. We live in the Now, but the best is yet to come.

Which of us can even begin to envision the blessed reality of our eternal home? We'll only see that when we awake in Christ's likeness.

Trying to describe heaven would be like trying to explain to a child in the womb what this world is like. That child cannot possibly understand when we say, "Wait till you see the green grass against a background of blue sky and fluffy white clouds. Wait till you feel the gentle rain on your face and smell the perfume of roses in June. Wait till you see the changing of Fall leaves into brilliant shades of orange, yellow and red, all of them blending together to cover the hills with a tapestry of fiery colors. Wait till you see the pure white snow covering the trees and bending its branches like a soft blanket in winter. Wait till you taste fresh strawberries, blueberries and Heath Bar Crunch ice cream."

The child might innocently respond with, "What is green, what is perfume or roses, what is rain or snow? What is Fall and what are leaves? I don't understand. What do you mean by taste?"

Try as you may to describe to that child an existence outside the womb, you will find no words to express or portray those things which are so familiar to you. In the same way, there are no words to describe what is waiting for the child of God on the other side of this world.

However, as it is written: *"No eye has seen, no ear has heard, no mind has conceived what God has prepared for those who love him."* (I Corinthians 2:9)

That ought to bring a smile to our faces. When our focus is on Christ and His unfailing promises everything else takes on a new dimension.

"For now we see in a mirror, dimly, but then face to face. Now I know in part, but then I shall know just as I also am known." (I Corinthians 13:12)

God does, however, give us an occasional glimpse into what He is lovingly preparing for us.

"In my Father's house are many mansions; if it were not so, I would have told you. I go to prepare a place for you." (John 14:2)

Reader, I don't know where you live today. I can tell you that, though I live in a most comfortable home, compared to ninety percent of the world's population, I absolutely do not live in a mansion. When the electrical power goes out in winter, the heat pump stops and my home gets cold. If I have too many guests at one time, the toilet will frequently overflow. If I forget to put the garbage out on pick-up day, my garage becomes a magnetic smorgasbord for flies. Now and then a little field mouse finds his way into my humble abode and sends me scurrying to set at least a dozen mouse traps until the tiny, pesky, uninvited guest is caught. Right now, the gutters on my roof need cleaning, the fence needs repair and the exterminator is here spraying for ants. This home was built with human hands, it's faulty, drafty, and costly.

But God, our God, He is the perfect architect of every priceless mansion in the Holy City. He's preparing mansions of peace, joy, love, and rest that will always remain. No one will lie awake worrying about developing a devastating illness. There will be no illness. No one will worry about an invasion from an enemy because there will be no enemies or weapons of destruction. There'll be no tears, no worries, and nothing and no one to fear.

"The eternal God will be our refuge and underneath the everlasting arms." (Deuteronomy 33:27)

"For our light and momentary troubles are achieving for us an eternal glory that far outweighs them all. So we fix our eyes not on what is seen, but on what is unseen. For what is seen is temporary, but what is unseen is eternal." (II Corinthians 4:17, 18)

"And God will wipe away every tear from their eyes; there shall be no more death, nor sorrow, nor crying. There shall be no more pain, for the former things have passed away." (Revelation 21:4)

Heaven will be a place of permanent relief from all the cares of this world. Having raised six children, I wiped away buckets of baby tears from little eyes for many years. But I have never been able to stop the surge of grown-up tears brought on by years of disappointments and broken dreams. From the beginning of time, a river of tears has been flowing on this earth, tears mingled with blood. Even the highest of religious or political leaders has not been able to stop the rapid, gushing flow, nor bind up the broken-hearted, nor set the captives free. Only the One who shed His own blood, his Holy, pure, precious blood to save us can do that. Only the spotless Lamb of God who willingly gave Himself for us, only He was worthy and able to open the gates of heaven so that we can freely enter His kingdom by His grace.

Jesus was sent specifically to bind up our wounds, to release us from darkness and set us free. Free from sin, fear, anxieties, guilt, deception, and anything else that binds us.

In the book of Luke in chapter four, we read that at the beginning of His ministry, Jesus went into the synagogue with some of His disciples. He was handed a scroll by one of the attendants. Jesus opened the scroll and began to read from the prophet Isaiah.

"The Spirit of the Lord God is upon me, because the Lord has anointed me to bring good news to the afflicted; He has sent me to bind up the brokenhearted, to set the captives free and release from darkness for the prisoners." (Isaiah 61:11)

When He finished reading, Jesus handed the scroll back to the attendant and announced to the congregation; *"Today, in your hearing, this Scripture has been fulfilled."* Clearly Jesus was saying that He is none other than Jeshua, Messiah, the Anointed One, the One promised through all the prophets. The One sent by the Father to redeem the lost.

"Truly, truly, I say to you, he who hears My Word, and believes Him who sent Me, has eternal life, and does not come into judgment, but has passed out of death into life." (John 5:24)

D. L. Moody told of an acquaintance whose only child had died. The accompanying sorrow was so great that his heart was almost broken. Before he suffered this loss, he had never given serious thought to life after death. Shortly after the child had been buried, the friends and relatives of the man were surprised to see the deep interest he began to show in the Bible. He read it continually. When someone asked him about his sudden interest in the sacred Book, he answered that he was trying to find out something about the place where his boy had gone. In the depth of his pain, the man had come to the only source of satisfaction and reliable information. An instant after death, the departed saint will know more about Heaven than all of the saints here on earth. But until we are called Home to be with the Lord, our knowledge is confined to what the Holy Spirit has revealed to us in the Bible.

The excitement of being ushered into our heavenly home by Jesus, our great High Priest, ought to fill us with such unbridled anticipation that all fear of death is removed. What spectacular joy awaits the child of God!

Humanity truly owes an enormous debt of gratitude for the simplicity of gaining eternity in Paradise. God, in His wisdom and mercy, did not make it complicated so that we should constantly be striving to be good enough, or try to fill a bottomless basket with good deeds in order to find favor with a Holy God. He did, however, make it very clear that salvation must be settled on this side of eternity. Heaven is freely given as a gift to those who wisely choose Him now.

"By grace you have been saved through faith; and that not of yourselves, it is the gift of God; not as a result of works, that no one should boast." (Ephesians 2:8, 9)

I recall, as a young child, trying to earn my way to Heaven, and being under the impression that if I visited the dead, I would receive a gold star beside my name in the heavenly ledger. Wishing to acquire as many stars as possible, I made it a practice to stop in at funeral parlors to visit corpses I knew nothing about.

There were a number of large funeral parlors within walking distance of my home, it was like living next to a gold mine. On a good day, I could find two or three occupied parlors in just one building. All the bleak-looking parlors with burning candles and tons of flowers bore wax-like figures with rosary beads intertwined between stiff fingers. Weeping relatives dressed in black from head to toe overflowed through the many corridors and into staircases as I wove my way from one room to another to accomplish my mission. I had work to do, accumulating stars was not an easy assignment.

My eyes were always on the lookout for a funeral crépe (floral arrangement), which might be hanging on the front door of a private home. The crépe indicated that a family member had died and the body was displayed in that home for anyone to freely walk in and view. That was an invitation to me to enter and kneel before the casket of a total stranger to say a quick prayer and walk out, leaving the parents wondering, *Who was that child?* I never enlightened them but only smiled, not knowing enough to even offer my condolences. I was not there for them, but for myself. After my solemn visits, I went skipping home, content in the fact that I had done my Christian duty like the obedient little child that I was.

Other times, I forced myself to walk gingerly between ghostly tombstones in Precious Blood Cemetery so I could pay my respects to the dearly departed whose names I could hardly pronounce. Most of them had been dead more years than I could even count. *"Today is my turn, tomorrow will be yours,"* read one gloomy epitaph that sent shivers up and down my spine.

My skinny little ten-year-old body was beginning to absorb the smell of carnations and give off the sickening aroma of death. But it was worth it to me because I was sure those gold stars had to be piling up as an enormous investment into my eternal reward. In the process of accumulating those valuable stars I had become a morbid ten-year-old professional mourner! I was literally chasing after gold stars hoping to someday trade in my prized collection for a golden crown covered with diamonds, sapphires, rubies, and pearls that would make Queen Elizabeth's crown look like the rhinestone ones I sometimes saw in the local Five & Ten cent store.

What a confusing maze of endless paths to nowhere we can follow if we don't know the scriptures or the power of God!

Jesus replied, "You are in error because you do not know the Scriptures or the power of God." (Matthew 22:29)

In this world, death is a part of living. It touches everyone's life and leaves us broken and scarred. It's a common enemy that no one escapes. But believers in Jesus have not been left to despair. We've been given precious promises and a bright hope for tomorrow. We have not been created for death but for everlasting life. Death is not the final insult as some have suggested but God's mercy and blessing, because it's only through death that we are ushered into glory.

It was sin that brought us to the edge of despair and it is God's grace that reunites us to the Father through Jesus who won the victory for us on the cross. That victory is ours when we come to Jesus in repentance. Whatever we may lose in the struggles of every day living, the Joy of the Lord is always there. It will never be taken away from us. We can sometimes hide that joy, but it's there for the taking. We need only to choose joy. It is a conscious choice that each individual makes.

There is cause for celebration as we join the long list of "Redeemed" of the Lord. We follow in the footsteps of Abraham, Moses, David, Mary, Joseph, and all the Apostles, and all the disciples throughout the ages. Followers of Jesus are a people of celebration!

As the triumphant song says; *"Oh, when the saints go marching in, I want to be there in that number when the saints go marching in."*

"But when this perishable will have put on the imperishable, and this mortal will have put on immortality, then will come about the saying that is written, 'Death is swallowed up in victory.' O death, where is your victory? O death, where is your sting?" (I Corinthians 15:54, 55)

We so often hear people refer to someone they loved as having 'passed away' but where have they passed away to? Some will tell you, based on their own conclusions that the person they loved so much has passed onto a higher level of existence somewhere in the great abyss. Others believe that after death one can return either in another body or even another form of life. That belief is in no way consistent or compatible with God's Word.

"Just as man is destined to die once, and after that to face judgement." (Hebrews 9:27)

Paul tells us in II Corinthians 5:8, that to be absent from the body is to be present with the Lord.

Jesus says His children have passed from death to life. We, who have accepted Christ as our Saviour are promised life forever in the kingdom of God, in the presence of the Glorious King of the universe Jesus is the way!

Jesus answered, "I am the way and the truth and the life. No one comes to the Father except through me." (John 14:6)

"There is a way that seems right to a man, but in the end it leads to death." (Proverbs 14:12)

"Whoever believes in the Son has eternal life, but whoever rejects the Son will not see life, for God's wrath remains on him." (John 3:36)

"And there is salvation in no one else; for there is no other name under heaven that has been given among men by which we must be saved." (Acts 4:12)

Based on the faithfulness of these precious promises, it is possible to have the joy of the Lord even in the midst of unspeakable tragedy. We need only to say, "Yes, Lord yes" and we're on our way to the greatest, most fulfilling adventure of all time.

Reader, have you secured your eternal salvation yet? Why would you hesitate when His love has made it so simple? Who knows what tomorrow will bring? Where will you spend eternity?

Where was God on September 11, 2001? He was in the same place that He was 2,000 years ago when His perfect, innocent Son was crucified in a very unjust and unwarranted act of terrorism. The Father was looking down from heaven with a broken heart. Tears were almost certainly pouring down His cheeks at the cruelty and hardness of man. His Word tells us that He is long-suffering. God suffered excruciating heartache as He watched His perfect and blameless Son hanging on a wooden cross, the symbol of shame normally reserved for criminals. In the same way, God suffered heartache on September 11, 2001, watching thousands of innocent people frantically searching for a way of escape from the intense smoke and fire waiting to consume them.

Daily He suffers as He calls out to his creation, *"Come to Me and I will give you rest!"* But, so often they turn a deaf ear and struggle to find peace and hope in all the wrong places. No, God did not desert Jesus on the cross, and He did not desert the people who were in the Twin Towers on September 11. Even as the smoke was rising,

He was still calling to them by name and extending His saving hand of mercy, forgiveness and redemption. He was ready then to welcome them into His eternal kingdom and He is still ready today, if only people will let Him.

"Trust in the Lord with all your heart and lean not on your own understanding; in all your ways acknowledge Him, and He will make your paths straight." (Proverbs 3:5, 6)

"For God so loved the world, that He gave His one and only Son, that whoever believes in Him, shall not perish but have eternal life. For God did not send His Son into the world to condemn the world, but to save the world through Him." (John 3:16, 17)

"Now is your time of grief, but I will see you again and you will rejoice, and no one will take away your joy." (John 16:22)

Home in Heaven

I am home in heaven, dear ones;
Oh, so happy and so bright.
There is perfect joy and beauty
In this everlasting light.

All the pain and grief is over,
Every restless tossing passed.
I am now at peace forever,
Safely home in heaven at last.

Did you wonder I so calmly
Trod the valley of the shade?
Oh, but Jesus' love illumined
Every dark and fearful glade.

And He came Himself to meet me
In the way so hard to tread;
And with Jesus' arm to lean on
Could I have one doubt or dread?

Then you must not grieve so sorely,
For I love you dearly still.
Try to look beyond death's shadows;
Pray to trust our Father's will.

There is work still waiting for you,
So you must not idly stand.
Do it now while life remaineth;
You shall rest in Jesus' land.

When that work is all completed,
He will gently call you home.
Oh, the rapture of that meeting;
Oh, the joy to see you come.

- Author Unknown